Version: 010720
Page Count: 168
ISBNs:
9781944607548 (Coil-Bound Print Book & PDF)
9781944607555 (Perfect-Bound Print Book)
9781944607562 (eBook)

Adobe RoboHelp 2019:
The Essentials (Second Edition)

Kevin Siegel

iCONLOGiC

"Skills and Drills" Learning

Rank Your Skills

Before starting this book, complete the skills assessment on the next page.

Skills Assessment

How This Assessment Works

Below you will find 10 course objectives for learning Adobe RoboHelp 2019. **Before starting this book**, review each objective and rank your skills using the scale next to each objective. A rank of ① means **No Confidence** in the skill. A rank of ⑤ means **Total Confidence**. After you've completed this assessment, work through the entire book. **After finishing the book**, review each objective and rank your skills now that you've completed the book. Most people see dramatic improvements in the second assessment after completing the lessons in this book.

Before Starting

1.	I can create topics.	①	②	③	④	⑤
2.	I can create TOC books.	①	②	③	④	⑤
3.	I can link topics together.	①	②	③	④	⑤
4.	I can create a style sheet (CSS).	①	②	③	④	⑤
5.	I can customize a Responsive HTML5 Preset.	①	②	③	④	⑤
6.	I can import Adobe Captivate Demos.	①	②	③	④	⑤
7.	I can create a Browse Sequence.	①	②	③	④	⑤
8.	I can create a Custom HTML Help Window.	①	②	③	④	⑤
9.	I can add images to a topic.	①	②	③	④	⑤
10.	I can Publish a project.	①	②	③	④	⑤

Now That I Am Finished

1.	I can create topics.	①	②	③	④	⑤
2.	I can create TOC books.	①	②	③	④	⑤
3.	I can link topics together.	①	②	③	④	⑤
4.	I can create a style sheet (CSS).	①	②	③	④	⑤
5.	I can customize a Responsive HTML5 Preset.	①	②	③	④	⑤
6.	I can import Adobe Captivate Demos.	①	②	③	④	⑤
7.	I can create a Browse Sequence.	①	②	③	④	⑤
8.	I can create a Custom HTML Help Window.	①	②	③	④	⑤
9.	I can add images to a topic.	①	②	③	④	⑤
10.	I can Publish a project.	①	②	③	④	⑤

IconLogic, Inc.
"Skills & Drills" Learning
Web: www.iconlogic.com
Email: info@iconlogic.com

"Skills and Drills" Learning

Contents

iCONLOGiC

"Skills and Drills" Learning

About This Book

This Section Contains Information About:

The Author

Kevin Siegel is a Certified Master Trainer (CMT), Certified Technical Trainer (CTT+), and Certified Online Training Professional (COTP). Following a successful tour of duty with the U.S. Coast Guard (where Kevin was twice decorated with the Coast Guard's Achievement Medal), he has spent decades as a technical communicator, classroom and online trainer, eLearning developer, publisher, and public speaker. Kevin, who founded IconLogic, Inc., in the early 1990s, has written hundreds of training books for adult learners. Some of his best-selling books include "Adobe Captivate: The Essentials," "Articulate Storyline: The Essentials," and "TechSmith Camtasia: The Essentials." Kevin has also been recognized by Adobe as one of the top trainers worldwide.

About IconLogic

Founded in 1992, IconLogic is a training, eLearning development, and publishing company offering services to clients across the globe.

As a training company, IconLogic has directly trained thousands of professionals both on-site and online on dozens of applications. As a publishing company, IconLogic has published hundreds of critically acclaimed books and created technical documents for both print and digital publication. And as a development company, IconLogic has produced content for some of the largest companies in the world, including Sanofi Pasteur, Kelsey Seybold, FAA, Office Pro, Duke Energy, Adventist Health System, AGA, PSA Air, AAA, Wells Fargo, American Express, Lockheed Martin, General Mills, Hagerty Insurance, Grange Insurance, Fannie Mae, ADP, ADT, World Bank, Heineken, EverFi, Bank of America, Fresenius Kabi, Wells Fargo, Federal Express, Fannie Mae, American Express, Microsoft, Department of For-Hire Vehicles, Federal Reserve Bank of Richmond, Walmart, Kroger, Duke Energy, USCG, USMC, Canadian Blood, Department of Homeland Security, Canadian Natural Resources, DC Child and Family Services, and the Department of Defense. You can learn more about IconLogic's varied services at www.iconlogic.com.

Book Conventions

Learners learn best by doing, not just by watching or listening. With that concept in mind, IconLogic books are created by trainers and authors with years of experience training adult learners. Each IconLogic book contains a minimal amount of text and is loaded with hands-on activities, screen captures, and challenge exercises to reinforce newly acquired skills.

This book is divided into modules. Because each module builds on lessons learned in a previous module, it is recommended that you complete each module in succession.

Here is the lesson key:

❏ instructions for you to follow look like this (the boxes are also used in bulleted lists)

If you are expected to type anything or if something is important, it is set in bold type like this:

❏ type **9** into the text field

If you are expected to press a key on your keyboard, the instruction looks like this:

❏ press [**shift**]

Software Updates and How They Affect This Book

With each major update of RoboHelp, my intention is to provide a book to support that version and make it available within 30-60 days of the software being released by Adobe. From time to time, Adobe releases updates for RoboHelp to fix bugs or add functionality. Usually, the updates are minor (bug fixes) and have little or no impact on the lessons in this book. However, Adobe could make significant changes to the way RoboHelp looks or behaves, even with a minor update.

This specific version of RoboHelp shown in this book is 2019.0.**10**. You can check your version by clicking the **Help** menu within RoboHelp 2019 (the version number is shown at the bottom of the Help menu). And you can check for updates by choosing **Help > Updates**.

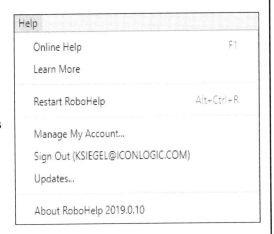

If something on your screen does not match what is shown in this book, please visit the RoboHelp 2019 book page on the IconLogic website for possible book updates or errata information (http://www.iconlogic.com/adobe-robohelp-2019-essentials-workbook.html) or email me at ksiegel@iconlogic.com.

> **Note:** At the time this book was written, there are two versions of RoboHelp 2019 available from **Adobe: 2019 *Classic*** and **Adobe RoboHelp 2019**. This book teaches you how to use **Adobe RoboHelp 2019**. Because RoboHelp 2019 *Classic* and RoboHelp 2019 are very different, you should not attempt to teach yourself RoboHelp 2019 Classic with this book. Instead, visit amazon.com and purchase my book titled *Adobe RoboHelp 2017 & 2019 Classic: The Essentials*.

Software Requirements For This Book

Prior to starting the lessons in this book, you will need Adobe RoboHelp 2019 (version 2019.0.10 or newer) installed on your computer. RoboHelp does not come with this book, nor can it be downloaded from the IconLogic website. You can purchase the program, or download a free 30-day trial version, from Adobe: www.adobe.com/products/robohelp.html.

Downloadable Book Assets (RoboHelp2019Data)

You're probably chomping at the bit, ready to dive into RoboHelp and begin creating awesome Help Systems. As you'll learn as you work through this book, all you need to create Help Systems on your own is Adobe RoboHelp and some content.

Wait, content? What content? You'll need text files, images, videos... the list of supporting assets you'll need to create even a basic Help System could go on and on. If you have never used RoboHelp before (and this book assumes that you have not), you cannot be expected to learn how to use RoboHelp on the fly as you come up with content. Learning by discovery is fine, but that takes (and possibly wastes) a lot of time.

I've got a better idea. You provide RoboHelp (the trial version is fine), and I'll provide all of the project files and supporting assets (such as content, images, and videos) to get you started.

Here are the steps you need to download the book's assets from the IconLogic website:

1. Start your web browser and go to the following web address:
   http://www.iconlogic.com/pc.htm.

2. Click the **RoboHelp 2019: The Essentials** link.

3. **Save** the zip file to your computer. (It's a good idea to note where the zip downloads so you can find it during the next step.)

   After the **RoboHelp2019Data.zip** file has fully downloaded, you can close the browser.

4. Find the **RoboHelp2019Data.zip** file you just downloaded and **unzip** it.

   Although you can unzip the assets anywhere on your computer, it's recommended that you keep the unzipped **RoboHelp2019Data** folder at the root of your hard drive (at **C:**) to match what is shown throughout this book.

Project Scenarios

During the activities that appear in this book, I'm going to ask you to use your imagination and pretend that you are a technical communicator for an awesome, but fictional, company called **Super Simplistic Solutions**. As a technical communicator, it is your job to create all of the documentation for the company's products, services, and internal policies and procedures.

During the lessons presented in this book, you will use Adobe RoboHelp 2019 to create a Policies and Procedures guide that can be used by employees via a desktop computer, a laptop, smart phone, or tablet.

Although the information you create in the upcoming policies guide is fictional, the content will likely seem similar to information in most corporate policy guides. Nevertheless, none of the information in the guide is based on real people, events, or companies. Any similarities are purely coincidental.

Confidence Checks

As you move through the lessons in this book, you will come across the little guy at the right. He indicates a Confidence Check. Throughout each module, you are guided through hands-on, step-by-step exercises. But at some point you'll have to fend for yourself. That is where Confidence Checks come in. Please be sure to complete each of the challenges because some exercises build on completed Confidence Checks.

Special Thanks

I wrote the first edition of this book based on early beta versions of RoboHelp 2019. Throughout the production cycle, the appearance and functionality of RoboHelp 2019 changed constantly. I truly appreciate the work of the proofreaders and beta testers who labored diligently to find as many typos, errors, and changes to the RoboHelp interface as possible. Specifically, I would like to thank **Peter Grainge**, **Nick Shears**, **Ellie Abrams**, **Mary Ann Hanlon**, **Matt Sullivan**, and **Nikki Williams** for their efforts.

Contacting IconLogic

Web: www.iconlogic.com
Email: ksiegel@iconlogic.com
Phone: 410.956.4949, ext 711

iCONLOGiC

"Skills and Drills" Learning

Module 1: Introduction to RoboHelp

In This Module You Will Learn About:

And You Will Learn To:

RoboHelp's History

According to Adobe, "RoboHelp is an easy-to-use authoring and publishing solution." Adobe also says that RoboHelp allows you to "deliver content to tablets, smartphones, and desktops using output formats such as Responsive HTML5."

Everything Adobe says about RoboHelp is true, and you'll see that for yourself as you work with RoboHelp via the lessons in this book.

I started using RoboHelp when it was owned by a company called Blue Sky Software. That company re-branded itself as eHelp Corporation. Later, eHelp was absorbed by Macromedia (of Dreamweaver and Director fame), which was, in turn, gobbled up by Adobe.

There have been several versions of RoboHelp over the years (see the table below). RoboHelp versions have included names like RoboHelp 5, 6, 7, 2002, X3, X4, and X5. RoboHelp 6 was Adobe's first RoboHelp version. However, eHelp Corporation also had a RoboHelp version 6. Yes, that's right. There was once eHelp RoboHelp 6, and there was an Adobe RoboHelp 6, creating a bit of customer confusion.

Starting with RoboHelp 2015, Adobe changed RoboHelp's naming convention again, this time using the year that the software version was released.

While this book focuses exclusively on RoboHelp 2019, update 10 and is titled, "Adobe RoboHelp 2019: The Essentials," RoboHelp 2019 is really RoboHelp version **23**. Update 10 of the software was released late in 2019.

Here is a list of RoboHelp versions and their release dates.

Version	Release date	Company/Note
1.0	January 1992	Blue Sky Software First generally-available version of RoboHelp
2.0–12.0	1993–2003	Blue Sky Software/eHelp Corporation
13.0	January 2004	Macromedia
14.0	January 2007	Adobe Systems, Inc.
15.0	September 2007	Adobe Systems, Inc.
16.0	January 2009	Adobe Systems, Inc.
17.0	January 2011	Adobe Systems, Inc.
18.0	July 2012	Adobe Systems, Inc.
19.0	January 2014	Adobe Systems, Inc.
20.0	June 2015	Adobe Systems, Inc.
21.0	January 2017	Adobe Systems, Inc.
22.0	August 2018	Adobe Systems, Inc.

Exploring RoboHelp

During the lessons in this module, I'm going to have you open a completed RoboHelp project, explore it a bit, and then generate outputs. As you move through subsequent modules in this book, you will learn how to build the completed project you're about to see from scratch.

Note: To complete the first activity below, you will need the RoboHelp2019Data folder on your computer (also known as data files or assets). If you have not already downloaded the data files to your hard drive, see **page ix** (in the About This Book section of this book) for instructions on the Downloadable Book Assets (RoboHelp2019Data). *The RoboHelp 2019 software is not included with this book. If you do not have RoboHelp 2019 installed on your computer, you can purchase the software, or download a 30-day trial, from Adobe at www.adobe.com/products/robohelp.html.*

Guided Activity 1: Open an Existing Project

1. Start Adobe RoboHelp 2019.

   After starting RoboHelp, the first thing you will see is the Starter Screen. From here, you can open Recent Projects, Create projects, and find additional Resources. (If the Starter is not on your screen, you can choose **View > Starter Screen** to view it.)

2. Open an existing project from the RoboHelp2019Data folder.

   ❑ on the **Starter Screen**, click **Open Project**

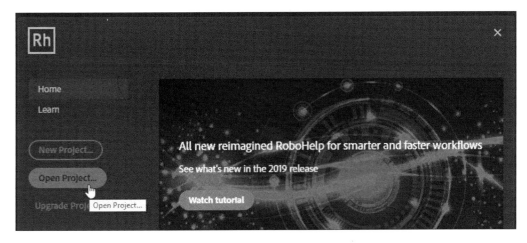

   ❑ navigate to and open the **RoboHelp2019Data** folder

   The RoboHelp2019Data folder contains several assets that support the lessons in this book including images, HTML files, a Word document, and existing RoboHelp projects. You'll be instructed when and how to use these assets as you move through the lessons in this book.

   ❑ open the **RoboHelpProjects** folder

   ❑ open the **completed_project** folder

   There are several subfolders within the completed_project folder. Cumulatively, all of the assets within those folders support the main RoboHelp project file (the project file's name is **completed_project.rhpj**).

   ❑ open **completed_project.rhpj**

The RoboHelp interface should look similar to the image below.

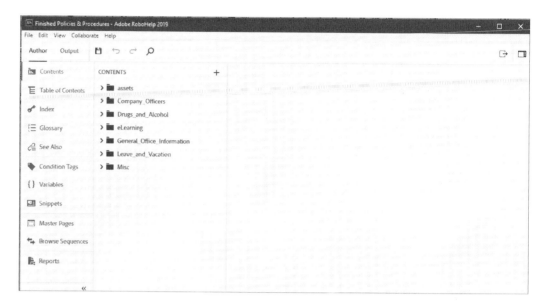

During the lessons presented throughout this book, you will learn how to create this project from scratch. From a scenario standpoint, you now work for a mythical company called **Super Simplistic Solutions**. You have been hired to create, among other things, the corporate policies and procedures guide. Rather than create the guide in a traditional word processor or desktop publishing application, you are going to create the guide in RoboHelp.

Before moving forward, I'd like to further explain the RoboHelp project file: the **rhpj** file you were instructed to open above. Although the rhpj file size is usually quite small, it's a powerful file with a critical job. The rhpj file controls the structure of the entire project (the project's folder structure, the TOCs, the Indexes, etc.). Although the rhpj file does not contain the Help System's content, it tracks where the content is stored, manages links, images, and controls a bunch of other behind the scenes functions.

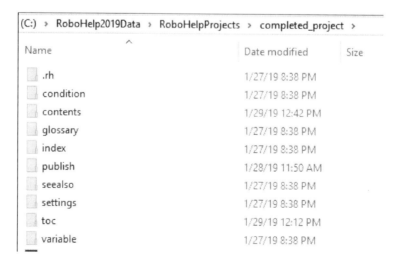

Guided Activity 2: Set the RoboHelp Application Theme

1. Ensure that the **completed_project** is still open. (If you're not sure how to open the RoboHelp project, see page 3.)

2. Change the Theme.

   ☐ choose **Edit > Preferences**

   The Application Settings dialog box opens. Changes you make here will affect all RoboHelp 2019 projects created or opened on your computer.

   ☐ at the **left** of the dialog box, select the **General** tab

   ☐ from the **Theme** drop-down menu, choose **Dark**

   The RoboHelp interface instantly switches from a light interface to dark. There are four RoboHelp Themes ranging from light to very dark. Personally, I like the contrast offered with the Dark Theme. The color scheme you use in RoboHelp is, of course, up to you.

   ☐ select any Theme that you like

   ☐ ensure that the remaining General settings match what is shown in the image below

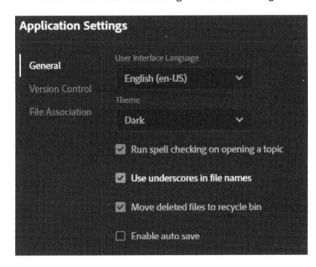

   ☐ click the **Done** button

Guided Activity 3: Explore Project Content

1. Ensure that the **completed_project** is still open. (If you're not sure how to open the RoboHelp project, see page 3.)

2. Observe the Author and Output areas.

   ❏ from the upper left of the RoboHelp interface, notice two tabs: **Author** and **Output**

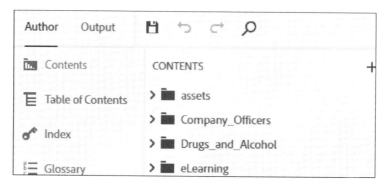

When you work in RoboHelp, you'll be wearing two hats: content creator and content generator. Much of what you need to create content for your Help System is found in the Author area. When you're done authoring content and you're ready to output content for your users, you'll use the Output area.

3. Open a topic.

   ❏ from the **Author** area, click **Contents** (if the Contents go away, click Contents again)

   ❏ from the **Contents** panel that appears, double-click the **General Office Information** folder (to expand the folder and see its topics)

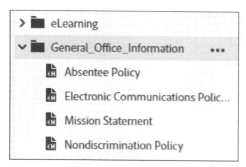

Note: If you see file names such as Electronic.htm instead of Electronic Communications Policy, choose **View > Show > Topics by Title**.

   ❏ from the list of items in the **General Office Information** folder, double-click **Mission Statement**

The topic opens in a panel to the right of Contents—the **Authoring Area**.

4. Open a second topic.

☐ from the **Contents** panel, open the **Drugs and Alcohol** folder

☐ double-click **Alcohol Policy**

Two topics are now open in the panel to the right of Contents. You'll be creating these topics in the new module.

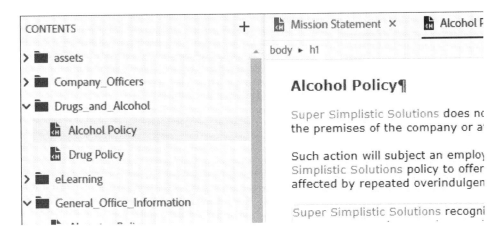

5. Switch between open topics.

☐ from above either open topic, click a topic's title tab to switch between the two topics

6. Close multiple topics.

☐ choose **File > Close All**

7. Close all expanded folders.

☐ on the **Contents** panel, right-click any folder and choose **Collapse All**

NOTES

Topics

You've likely heard the saying that content is king. It's true. The heart of any Help System is its content and the information it provides. Most of the content in RoboHelp is contained within topics. Topics typically consist of text formatted with styles (page 39), images (page 68), hyperlinks (page 59), videos (page 77), tables (page 102), and more. In the next few activities, you'll create a topic, edit it a bit, and then delete it.

Guided Activity 4: Create, Edit, and Delete a Topic

1. Ensure that the **completed_project** is still open. (If you're not sure how to open the RoboHelp project, refer to page 3.)

2. Create a topic.

   ☐ on the **Contents** panel, right-click beneath the last folder

   ☐ choose **New > New Topic**

   The New Topic dialog box opens.

   ☐ change the **Title** to **My First Topic**

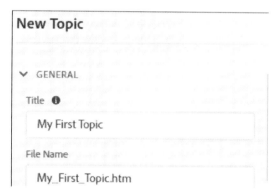

   ☐ from the bottom of the dialog box, click the **Create** button

   The new topic appears on the Content panel and opens for editing.

3. Edit the new topic.

   ☐ in the space below the heading, type: **The best Help topic will contain only enough text to get my point across and no more. One paragraph or two is ideal, supported by an image or two.**

Observe the asterisk to the right of the topic's title. 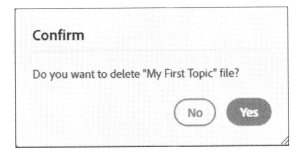 The asterisk indicates an unsaved topic.

4. Save and close the topic.

   ☐ choose **File > Save**

   ☐ choose **File > Close**

5. Delete a topic.

   ☐ on the **Contents** panel, right-click the **My First Topic** topic and choose **Delete**

You will be asked to confirm the action.

Confirm

Do you want to delete "My First Topic" file?

(No) (Yes)

   ☐ click the **Yes** button

Adding and Deleting Topics Confidence Check

1. Create a new topic titled **My Second Topic**.

2. Change the title of the new topic to **Delete Me**.

3. Delete the **Delete Me** topic.

NOTES

TOCs and Indexes

When users access your published Help content, they'll typically rely on a Table of Contents (TOC) to understand the structure or logic behind the Help System. Users rely on an Index to quickly find content (just as you might do when reading a reference guide). This project already has both a TOC and an Index. You will learn how to create both during lessons presented later in this book.

Guided Activity 5: Explore a TOC and an Index

1. Ensure that the **completed_project** is still open.

2. Open an existing TOC.

   ☐ from the panel at the far left, click **Table of Contents**

   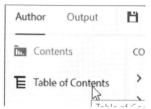

   This project contains one TOC named **policies**.

   ☐ double-click **policies** to open the TOC

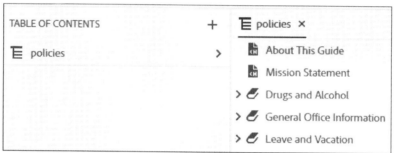

You will learn how to create this Table of Contents beginning on page 34.

3. Open an existing Index.

   ☐ from the panel at the far left, click **Index**

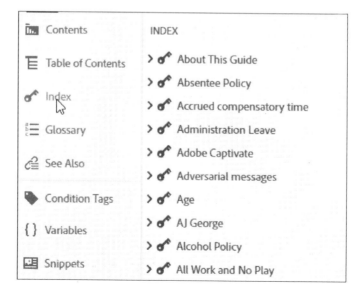

You will learn how to create this Index beginning on page 107.

Outputs

If you'd like to get a sense of what your users will experience when accessing your published Help System, you need to generate output files from your project assets. **Your users do not need RoboHelp** to open output you create with RoboHelp. However, depending upon the type of output you generate, the users' hardware and software requirements will vary.

RoboHelp's outputs, located in the Output panel at the top left of the RoboHelp window, contains several presets. Arguably, the most commonly used outputs are **Responsive HTML5**, **Frameless**, and **Microsoft HTML Help**.

Microsoft HTML Help

Microsoft HTML Help (HTML Help for short) is the oldest of the outputs. When you generate HTML Help, RoboHelp creates a single, compressed CHM file (pronounced "chum"). A CHM file works great if your users are accessing the published Help System with a Windows-based PC and if the CHM file is installed on the user's hard drive. CHM files do not work if your users access the Help System with a computer or laptop running iOS, or if the user is on a mobile device such as a tablet or smart phone. Nor do CHM files work well if opened by users via a server. Last, but not least, you are limited by how much you can customize the look and feel of the generated HTML Help window.

Given all the negative stuff I just wrote above, you might think that HTML Help is a layout that is best avoided. Not necessarily. There is much to like about this output. For instance, HTML Help files are self-contained Help Systems (you don't need other programs to use them outside of what is already installed on most Windows-based computers). And CHM files are typically much, much smaller than any of the other layouts. The savings in size alone is one reason that many people rely on CHM files, even given their inherent limitations.

Guided Activity 6: Generate Microsoft HTML Help

1. Ensure that the **completed_project** is still open.

2. Generate the Microsoft HTML Help Layout.

   ❏ from the upper left of the RoboHelp window, click **Output**

   ❏ click **Output Presets**

   ❏ from among the **Output Presets**, double-click **Microsoft HTML Help** to open the preset for editing

   ❏ select the **General** category

   ❏ from the **Output Path** area, click the **Browse** icon

   ❏ browse to **RoboHelp2019Data > output > HTML_Help** and then click the **Select Folder** button

   Note: Depending upon where your **RoboHelp2019Data** is stored, the path shown in the image below may not exactly match your path to your **HTML_Help** output folder.

Output Path

C:/RoboHelp2019Data/output/HTML_Help/

3. Close the Microsoft HTML Help Preset by clicking the X as shown in the image below (save if prompted).

4. Generate the Output.

   ☐ from among the **Output Presets**, right-click **Microsoft HTML Help** and choose **Generate**

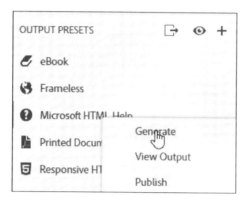

Because the project is small, generating the layout takes only seconds.

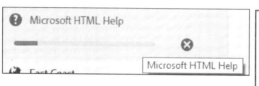
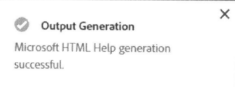

5. View the Output.

   ☐ right-click **Microsoft HTML Help** and choose **View Output**

This is a finished Help System and is exactly what an end-user will should they have access to the output.

The puzzle piece in the **Our Mission** topic is a special kind of image known as an image map. When you click the different puzzle pieces, you'll be taken to topics throughout the Help System.

You'll learn how to create topic-to-topic links on page 59 and image maps on page 74.

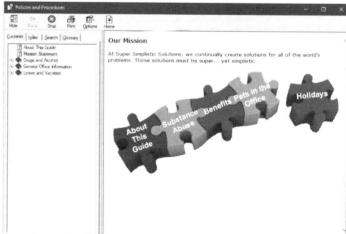

Microsoft HTML Help Output Confidence Check

1. Notice that the TOC in the HTML Help window is the same TOC you explored a moment ago within RoboHelp.

2. Open the **General Office Information** book.

3. Spend the next few moments selecting the pages you find inside the book.

4. Select the Index tab and notice that this is the same Index that you explored in RoboHelp a moment ago.

5. Close the Help window and minimize RoboHelp.

6. Using Windows Explorer, open the **RoboHelp2019Data** folder.

7. Open the **outputs** folder and then open the **HTML_Help** folder.

   Within the HTML_Help folder, you'll find the generated help file: policies.chm. Everything the Help System needs to work on your user's computer is included in this one highly compressed CHM file.

8. Double-click the CHM file to open the generated Help System.

policies.chm

9. Close the Help Window and return to the RoboHelp project.

Frameless Output

You generated Microsoft HTML Help during the last activity. Although Microsoft HTML Help results in the fewest and smallest output files to manage (a single CHM file), CHM files are limited in many ways (see page 11).

As an alternative to HTML Help, Frameless output can be viewed on the web or using a desktop application. This output type works with any web browser and platform and is highly customizable. One of the downsides of Frameless is the large number of files that are output when you generate. Remember that Microsoft HTML Help output is just one file. When you generate Frameless, you could potentially be generating thousands of codependent files that must always be kept together to ensure that the Help System works as expected. The other major downside of Frameless is that it doesn't support mobile devices. (To support mobile users, you need to output Responsive HTML5, which you'll learn about on page 15).

Guided Activity 7: Generate Frameless Output

1. Ensure that the **completed_project** is still open.

2. Generate and view Frameless output.

   ☐ from among the **Output Presets**, double-click **Frameless** to open the preset for editing

   ☐ select the **General** category

   ☐ from the **Output Path** area, click the **Browse** icon

   ☐ browse to and select: **RoboHelp2019Data > output > Frameless**

Output Path
C:/RoboHelp2019Data/output/Frameless/

   ☐ save the Preset (via **File > Save All**)

   ☐ right-click the **Frameless** output and choose **Generate**

   ☐ right-click the **Frameless** output and choose **View Output**

The Help System opens within your computer's default web browser.

I personally love the look of the Frameless output (keep in mind that it's very customizable).

I also love how the content wraps nicely as the browser window is resized (as shown in the image at the right).

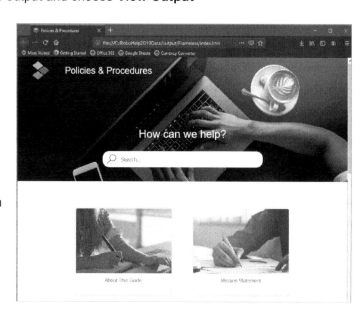

3. Close the browser window and return to RoboHelp.

Responsive HTML5 Output

The sale of smartphones is exceeding the sale of traditional phones; the sale of tablets exceeds those of desktop computers. This trend has led to a need for help authors to create content that can be accessed from both mobile devices and desktop computers.

When you output Responsive HTML with RoboHelp, just about everything in the Help window reflows, resizes, and adjusts to provide optimal viewing across a wide range of devices and screen sizes.

Guided Activity 8: Generate Responsive HTML5 Output

1. Ensure that the **completed_project** is still open.

2. Generate and view Responsive HTML5 output.

   ☐ from among the **Output Presets**, double-click **Responsive HTML5** to open it for editing

   ☐ select the **General** category

   ☐ from the **Output Path** area, click the **Browse** icon

   ☐ browse to and select: **RoboHelp2019Data > output > Responsive_HTML**

   Output Path

   C:/RoboHelp2019Data/output/Responsive_HTML/

   ☐ save the Preset (via **File > Save All**)

   ☐ right-click the **Responsive HTML5** output and choose **Generate**

   ☐ right-click the **Responsive HTML5** output and choose **View Output**

3. Resize the browser window.

   Notice that the layout changes (responds) as you resize the browser window.

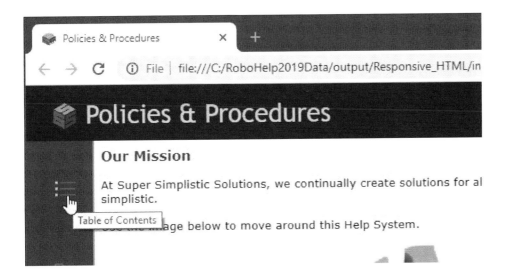

4. Close the browser window and return to the RoboHelp project.

Printed Documentation Output

So far you have generated output specifically for use onscreen (desktop, laptop... even mobile). Certainly, users can print any topic while it's onscreen. However, if you'd like to create a print-ready version of your Help System, the Print Documentation output is the way to go.

Guided Activity 9: Generate a PDF Version of the Help System

1. Ensure that the **completed_project** is still open.

2. Output a PDF.

   ❏ from the panel at the left, **Output** area, **Output Presets**, double-click **Printed Documentation**

   ❏ select the **General** category

   ❏ from the **Output Path** area, click the **Browse** icon

   ❏ browse to and select: **RoboHelp2019Data > output > Printed_Documentation**

   Output Path

   C:/RoboHelp2019Data/output/Printed_Documentation/

   ❏ save the Preset (via **File > Save All**)

   ❏ right-click the **Printed Documentation** Preset and choose **Generate**

   ❏ right-click the **Printed Documentation** Preset and choose **View Output**

   The PDF opens in Adobe Reader, Acrobat, or the default PDF reader software on your computer.

3. Close the PDF and return to the RoboHelp project.

eBook Output

During the last activity you created a print document out of a Help System. You could send the print documentation to your users, and using Adobe Reader, they could open the PDF, read it, and print it. Most mobile devices can open a PDF, but the small display common on smart phones and smaller tablets makes reading the PDF a challenge.

Instead of a PDF, you can use RoboHelp to generate an eBook (also known as an electronic publication) using your existing Help System. The advantage of the eBook format over PDF technology is mainly readability. When opened with an eBook reader, the text always wraps to fit the size of the user's device or display, and the user can control the font, font size, and color. Although the eBook format is flexible, it does not currently support all of the bells and whistles that you can add to a RoboHelp project. For instance, eBook readers do not support expanding hotspots, glossaries, or interactive eLearning videos. (You'll learn how to add these features later in this book.)

Note: In the steps that follow, you will use RoboHelp to generate an eBook file. After the eBook file has been created, you will need an eBook reader on your computer to open the eBook file. Although there are many eBook readers (some free, some not), Adobe has a free eBook reader called Adobe Digital Editions (http://www.adobe.com/products/digitaleditions). For more information on the eBook format, visit **https://www.w3.org/publishing/**.

Guided Activity 10: Output an eBook

1. Ensure that the **completed_project** is still open.

2. Output an eBook.

   ❏ from among the **Output Presets**, double-click **eBook** to open it

   ❏ select the **General** category

   ❏ from the **Output Path** area, click the **Browse** icon

   ❏ browse to and select: **RoboHelp2019Data > output > ePub**

   ❏ save the Preset (via **File > Save All**)

   ❏ right-click the **eBook** Preset and choose **Generate**

   ❏ right-click the **eBook** Preset and choose **View Output**

   The eBook opens in your computer's default ePub reader. In the image at the right, you can see a page from the ePub as it appears using Books for the Mac.

3. Close the eBook file.

4. Return to RoboHelp and close the Project.

Pets in the Office Policy

Pets... we love them. As a Super Simplistic Solutions employee, you are permitted to bring your pet to work every Friday, provided your pet is not on the banned list below and you follow a few, simple rules.

A Few Simple Rules

- Your pet bites, we bite you... and you pay the piper

- Your pet poops in the office, you clean it up immediately

- Just say NO to barking!!!!

Notes

iCONLOGiC
"Skills and Drills" Learning

Module 2: Creating Projects

In This Module You Will Learn About:

- New Projects, page 20
- Topics, page 23
- Importing Content, page 27
- Source View, page 30

And You Will Learn To:

- Create a Blank Project, page 20
- Create a New Topic, page 23
- Rename and Delete Topics, page 25
- Import HTML Files, page 27
- Import Word Documents, page 28
- Edit Text Formatting in Source View, page 30

New Projects

During the last module, you opened and explored an existing project. That module was designed to get you comfortable with the RoboHelp interface. Now that you know your way around RoboHelp a bit more, let's create a blank project that will become the Policies & Procedures guide for your mythical employer, Super Simplistic Solutions. The new project you create will have humble beginnings. It will not have much structure or content. However, as you work through the modules in this book, your project will evolve. In the end, your project will contain plenty of content, graphics, multiple forms of navigation, and many of the same type of high-end features you saw when you explored the project in the last module.

Guided Activity 11: Create a Blank Project

1. Create a Blank Project.

    ☐ choose **File > New Project** (or click **New Project** on the **Starter Screen**)

    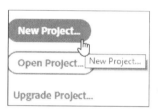

    Note: If the Starter Screen is not currently open, choose **View > Starter Screen** to open it.

    The New Project dialog box opens.

    ☐ in the **Title** field, type **Policies & Procedures**

    ☐ ensure that the **Language** is **English (US)**

    ☐ from the **Save location** area, click the **Select Folder** icon

    Note: You should have already downloaded and unzipped the RoboHelp2019Data folder to your hard drive as instructed in the "About This Book" section of this book (see page ix).

    ☐ navigate to and open the **RoboHelp2019Data** folder

    ☐ click once on the **RoboHelpProjects** folder and then click the **Select Folder** button

    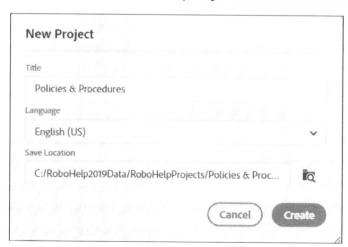

    ☐ click the **Create** button

Your new RoboHelp project opens. By default, the project contains a single topic titled **First Topic.** If necessary, select **Author** from the left of the RoboHelp window and then select **Contents** to see the lone topic. Next, you'll change the default topic's Title, File Name, and add some content to it.

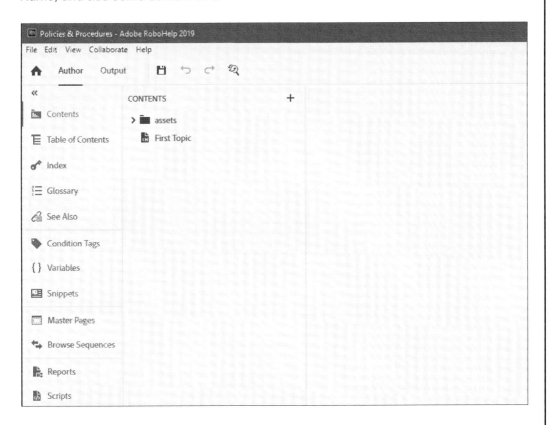

2. Change a topic's Title and File Name.

    ☐ from the **Contents** area, right-click the **First Topic** and choose **Properties**

    The Topic Properties dialog box opens.

    ☐ change the topic's **Title** to **Mission Statement**
    ☐ change the topic's **File Name** to **mission**

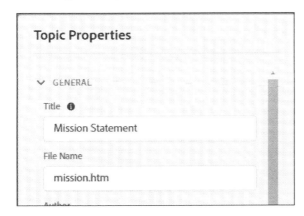

Note: You can elect to use upper or lowercase letters in file names. Some organizations require the use of one or the other (lowercase is the most common).

Every topic in your project has two names: Title and File Name. The title is seen by your users. It can and should contain spaces and can be descriptive. By contrast, a topic's File Name is not seen by the user. The name should not contain spaces or special characters. Also note that the .htm extension is added to the file name automatically by RoboHelp.

❏ click the **Apply** button

3. Add topic content.

   ❏ from among the **Contents**, double-click the **Mission Statement** topic to open it for editing

   ❏ replace the heading text with **Our Mission**

   ❏ highlight the remaining text in the topic and replace it with:
   To continually create solutions for all of the world's problems. Those solutions must be super... yet simplistic.

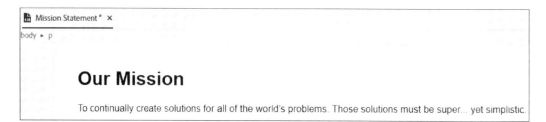

4. Save the project.

   ❏ from above the **Contents** area, click **Save All** 💾

   When you work within RoboHelp, multiple assets might be open at one time. For instance, it's possible to have several topics open, all in an unsaved state. As you make changes to project assets, the project file (project name.rhpj) also remains in an unsaved state. For that reason, it's a good idea to use the Save All option frequently. Alternatively, you can press [**ctrl**] [**s**] on your keyboard.

5. Close the Mission Statement topic.

   ❏ at the right of the topic's title, click the **X**

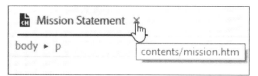

You are about to learn how to create topics on-the-fly. Because RoboHelp allows you to have multiple topics open and switch among them by clicking a topic's tab, it's not necessary to close topics prior to creating new topics or editing existing topics. From this point forward, you can close topics (or not) as you see fit.

Topics

Your new project contains just a single topic (Mission Statement). In the next few activities, you will learn how to create, rename, and delete topics. Each new RoboHelp topic you create is actually an HTML file. As I promised in the first module of this book, you do not need to know HTML to create HTML topics.

Guided Activity 12: Create a New Topic

1. Create a new topic.

   ☐ still working in your new **Policies & Procedures** project, at the right of the **Contents** area, click the **New File/Folder** icon ➕

   ☐ choose **New Topic**

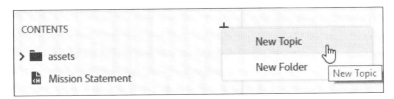

The New Topic dialog box opens.

   ☐ change the Topic Title to **Philosophy**

The Title is the most important part of a topic. A good title precisely describes what the topic is about: whether it explains a concept or provides instructions on getting something done. Titles are shown in search results and users decide a topic's worth based on the title. Search engines like Google and RoboHelp's own search select pages for a large part on the title. A bad title means that users might not find the help they need.

Notice that a File Name (Philosophy.htm) has been automatically added to the File Name field that mimics the Topic Title you typed. As you create topics, keep in mind that you can give a topic just about any title you want. Because users see titles, I encourage Help authors to be descriptive when creating Topic Titles. You can use one word, multiple words, spaces, and punctuation in Topic Titles. However, File Names are not as flexible. You cannot use spaces or special characters in File Names. If you want to create a topic with multiple words in its title, RoboHelp will automatically replace those spaces with underscores. You can always edit both the Title and File Name at any time via a topic's Properties dialog box (you'll learn how on page 25).

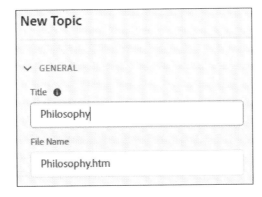

   ☐ click the **Create** button

2. Add content to the new Philosophy topic.

☐ with the new Philosophy topic open for editing, replace the existing heading text with **Super Simple Tactics...**

☐ press [**enter**]

☐ type **Tactics that focus on motivation, engagement, relevance and usability are standard operating procedures for all of our projects. Working with subject matter experts, we distill and render technical content in logical and easily digestible units. We link concept and application to the real world, with a user-centered perspective.**

RoboHelp assumes that the text you just typed is supposed to be formatted as a standard paragraph (as opposed to heading text like the first paragraph). In this instance, RoboHelp made a good assumption. Soon enough you'll learn that it's pretty easy to change the appearance of any topic text via Styles.

Super Simple Tactics...

Tactics that focus on motivation, engagement, relevance and usability are standard operating procedures for all of our projects. Working with subject matter experts, we distill and render technical content in logical and easily digestible units. We link concept and application to the real world, with a user-centered perspective.

---

3. Save the project.

☐ from above the **Contents** area, click **Save All** 💾 (or press [**ctrl**] [**s**] on your keyboard)

Guided Activity 13: Rename and Delete Topics

1. Create a new topic.

   ☐ still working in your new **Policies & Procedures** project, at the right of the Contents area, click **New File/Folder** (the plus sign)

   ☐ choose **New Topic**

   The New Topic dialog box opens.

   ☐ change the Topic Title to **Ooops**

   ☐ confirm the File Name is **Ooops.htm**

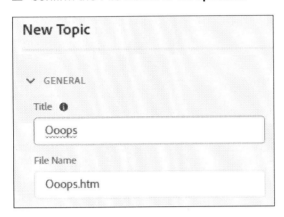

   ☐ click the **Create** button

2. Rename a topic's Title and File Name.

   ☐ from the **Contents** area, right-click **Ooops** and choose **Properties**

   The Topic Properties dialog box opens.

   ☐ change the Topic Title to **Delete Me**

   Notice that the topic's File Name does not automatically change.

   ☐ change the File Name to **Delete_Me**

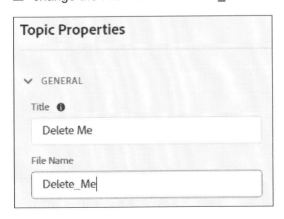

   ☐ click the **Apply** button

Because you are viewing the contents by Title, the update to the Title appears in the Contents area after you Apply the changes. (You can switch to File Name view by choosing **View > Show > Topics by Title** to toggle the option **off**. If you do so now, just remember to toggle Topic by Title back on so your screen matches the images shown in this book.)

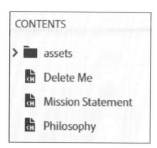

3. Delete a topic.

☐ from the Contents area, right-click the **Delete Me** topic and choose **Delete**

You will be asked to confirm the deletion.

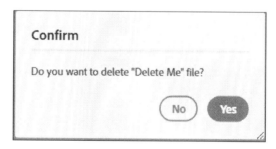

☐ click the **Yes** button

Importing Content

You can import several types of existing documents into a RoboHelp project including HTML files, Microsoft Word documents (docx files), and Adobe FrameMaker documents. If the imported documents contain images or videos, those assets will also be imported.

Guided Activity 14: Import HTML Files

1. Ensure that the **Policies & Procedures** project is still open.

2. Import an HTML file.

   ☐ from the **Contents** area, right-click beneath the **Philosophy** topic and choose **Import > HTML Topic**

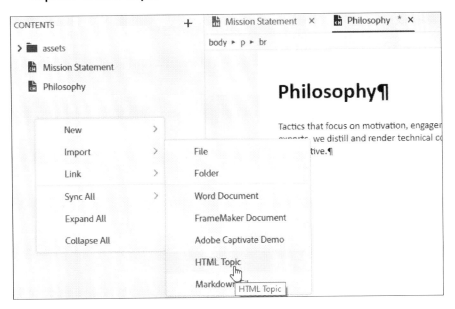

   ☐ from the **RoboHelp2019Data** folder, open the **content** folder

   There are several HTML files in the folder.

   ☐ select **absence.htm**
   ☐ click the **Open** button

   The **Absentee Policy** topic is imported and is listed with the other project topics.

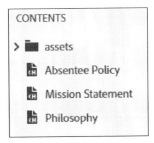

Guided Activity 15: Import Word Documents

1. Ensure that the **Policies & Procedures** project is still open.

2. Import a Word document.

   ☐ click in the bottom of the **Contents** area (to deselect any folders)

   ☐ choose **File > Import > Word Document**

   ☐ at the right of the **Word Document** area, click the **Select** icon 🔍

   ☐ from the **RoboHelp2019Data** folder, open the **content** folder

   ☐ open **SubstanceAbuse.docx**

3. Control how the Word content is split into new topics.

   ☐ from the **Start new topic from style** area, choose **Heading 1** drop-down menu

   The document you are importing contains two paragraphs that are using Word's Heading 1 style. During the import process, the single Word document will be split into two RoboHelp topics.

Start new topic from style :
Word Style
Select Style ⌄
Heading1 ✕

   ☐ click the **Import** button

   On the **Contents** area, there are two new topics (Alcohol Policy and Drug Policy) instead of a single topic named SubstanceAbuse. RoboHelp created the two topics because Heading 1 is being used in the SubstanceAbuse document twice.

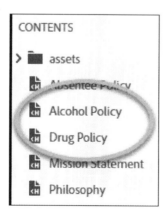

Importing Content Confidence Check

1. Import the following HTML files into your project. (You can import several HTML files at one time by [**shift**]-clicking to select contiguous files or [**ctrl**]-clicking to select noncontiguous files and then clicking **Open**.)

   overtime.htm, payroll.htm, pets.htm, purpose.htm, special.htm, and **term.htm**

   Import the following Word documents into your project. (While importing, use **Heading 1** to create new topics.)

   Electronic, Leave, Nondiscrimination, and **Vacation**

   You should now have up to 15 topics in your project.

2. Change the Title of the **Leave** topic to **Leave Policy**. (You learned how to change a topic's Title on page 25.)

3. Change the Title of the **General Office Information** topic to **Overtime Policy**.

4. Change the Title of **Payroll** topic to **Payroll Policy**.

5. Change the Title of the **PURPOSE** topic to **About This Guide**.

6. Change the Title of **401(k) Plan** topic to **Special Benefits**.

7. Change the Title of the **Termination of Employment** topic to **Termination Policy**.

8. Save the project.

   Note: You are currently viewing content by topic Title. If you prefer, you can switch the view so you can see the topic list by file name by choosing **View > Show** and deselecting Topics by Title.

NOTES

Source View

Although it is not necessary for you to know HTML to create RoboHelp projects, knowing a little HTML can pay off when imported content causes trouble because of misplaced or missing HTML tags. During the steps that follow, you will import a topic and use RoboHelp's Source View to edit the appearance of topic text.

Guided Activity 16: Edit Text Formatting in Source View

1. Ensure that the **Policies & Procedures** project is still open.

2. Import the HTML Topic **conflict.htm** from the **RoboHelp2019Data > content** folder.

    The imported topic is titled **Conflict Resolution Policy**.

3. Open the **Conflict Resolution Policy** topic for editing.

4. Use Source View to change the appearance of text from bold to italic.

    ❑ from the upper right of the RoboHelp window, click the **Source View** icon

    ❑ in line **12**, replace the **<b>** with **<i>**

    ```
    disrupt the mission and values
    <p><i>Conflict Resolution:</i> F
    grievance or concern will be re
    ```

    The <b> tags change the style of text to **bold**; <i> is the HTML tag for *italic*.

    ❑ from the upper right of the RoboHelp window, click the **Author** icon

    In the fourth paragraph, the phrase **Conflict Resolution**, which was bold, is now italicized.

    ```
    Conflict Resolution: Followin
    individuals who have a grieva
    requested to take their concer
    ```

Source View Confidence Check

1. Using Source View, change the appearance of the phrase Conflict Resolution back to bold.

    ```
    has the potential to disrupt the
    <p><b>Conflict Resolution:</b> Fo
    requested to take their concern
    ```

2. Save and close the Conflict Resolution Policy topic.

3. Close the project by choosing **File > Close Project**.

iCONLOGiC
"Skills and Drills" Learning

Module 3: Project Structure, TOCs, and Styles

In This Module You Will Learn About:

And You Will Learn To:

Project Structure

Creating folders and subfolders in the Contents area can help you organize your project's topics, images, and other assets. Folders make it easier to access and edit your content as your Help project grows and becomes more sophisticated. As an added bonus, the folder structure you create can be re-purposed and used to automatically create a Table of Contents (TOC). It's a nifty process you'll come to appreciate later in this module.

Guided Activity 17: Create Project Folders

1. Open an existing RoboHelp project.

   ☐ choose **File > Open Project**

   ☐ from the **RoboHelp2019Data** folder, open the **RoboHelpProjects** folder

   ☐ open the **project_structure_css** folder

   ☐ open **project_structure_css.rhpj**

   This project is similar to the project you were working on during the last module.

2. Create a folder.

   ☐ at the right of the **Contents** area, click the **New File/Folder** icon ➕

   ☐ choose **New Folder**

   The New Folder dialog box opens.

   ☐ change the name to **General Office Information**

   Because folder names cannot contain spaces, the spaces you typed are automatically replaced with underscores: **General_Office_Information**.

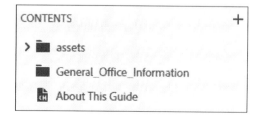

   ☐ click the **Done** button

   The folder is added to your list of Contents.

   CONTENTS   +
   > 📁 assets
      📁 General_Office_Information
      📄 About This Guide

3. Move a topic into a project folder.

☐ on the **Contents** area, drag the **About This Guide** topic **up** and **into** the **General_Office_Information** folder

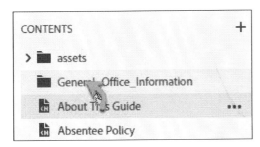

If you expand the **General_Office_Information** folder you see the relocated topic.

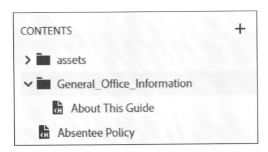

Project Structure Confidence Check

1. Create a new folder named **Drugs and Alcohol**.

2. Create a new folder named **Leave_and_Vacation**.

3. Add topics to the project folders as necessary to match the pictures below.

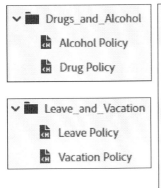

Table of Contents

A typical Help System has a Contents tab that you create in the Table of Contents area of the Author tab. A typical Contents tab is made up of books and pages but can also include Placeholders and Merged Projects. Books can contain pages or other books. TOC pages typically point to project topics.

Guided Activity 18: Create a TOC Book

1. Ensure that you are still working in the **project_structure_css** project.

2. Open a Table of Contents.

   ☐ from the far left of the RoboHelp window, click **Table of Contents**

   There is a default Table of Contents called **Default**. You can edit the default or create your own. You will work with new TOCs later in this book. For now, let's edit the default.

3. Remove a page from the default TOC.

   ☐ from within the **Table of Contents** area, double-click the **Default** TOC to open it for editing

   ☐ right-click the **First Topic** page in the default TOC and choose **Delete**

   Because you are not deleting content from the project but rather deleting a reference that is pointing to existing content, you are not prompted to confirm the deletion.

4. Add a book to the default Table of Contents.

❑ from the top of the **Default** TOC, click the **New Book** icon

The Insert Book dialog box opens.

❑ in the **Title** area, type **Book 1**

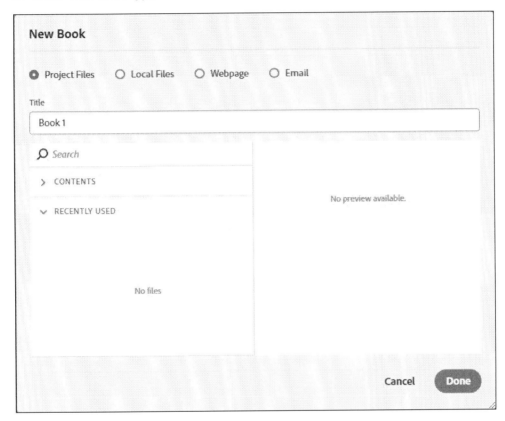

New Book

⦿ Project Files   ○ Local Files   ○ Webpage   ○ Email

Title

Book 1

🔍 Search

> CONTENTS

⌄ RECENTLY USED

No preview available.

No files

Cancel   Done

❑ click the **Done** button

The Default TOC now contains a single book. The book is not currently pointing toward any existing content.

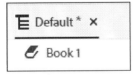

5. Add a page to Book 1 on the TOC.

☐ from the left of the RoboHelp window, click **Contents**

☐ from the **Contents** area, open the **Drugs and Alcohol** folder

☐ drag **Alcohol Policy** topic directly on top of **Book 1**

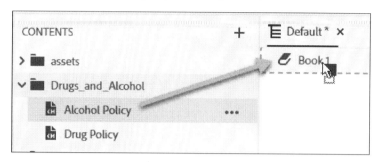

☐ drag the **Drug Policy** topic directly on top of **Book 1**

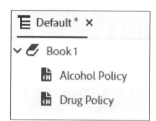

TOC Books Confidence Check

1. Add three more books to the TOC named **Book 2**, **Book 3**, and **Book 4** that point to any topic.

2. For each of your new books, add a few pages.

3. Use the **Move** icons at the top of the TOC as necessary to ensure your books are structured similarly to what is shown in the second image below.

Note: You're not going to be keeping the TOC very long, so you don't have to perfectly match your work to the image.

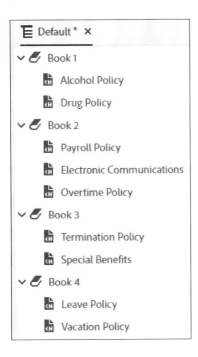

4. Save the project.

Automatic TOCs

During the last activity, you learned how to build a TOC from scratch. However, if you have already spent time creating some structure for the Contents (which you did at the beginning of this module when you created the three folders), you can leverage RoboHelp's ability to automatically create a TOC based on that existing structure.

Guided Activity 19: Auto-Create a TOC

1. Ensure that the Default TOC is still **open**.

2. Auto-create a TOC based on existing folders.

   ❐ from the top of the **TOC**, click the **Auto-create TOC** icon

   The Confirm dialog box opens.

   ❐ select **Delete current TOC before creating new**

   Delete current TOC before creating new removes the existing TOC you created. **Create TOC pages for mid-topic links (bookmarks)** is an optional setting. You haven't yet learned how to create bookmarks (you will during the activity on page 62). Because your current project does not contain any bookmarks, it does not matter if you select the option or not.

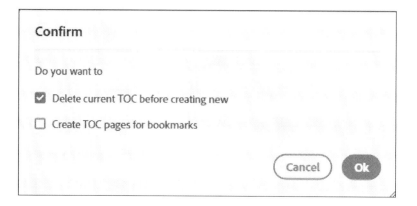

   ❐ click the **OK** button

   The content you originally added to the policies TOC is replaced by books and pages that match the structure you set up in the Contents area.

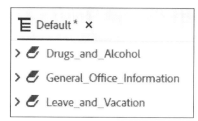

3. Save the project.

Guided Activity 20: Edit Book Names and Reorder Book Pages

1. Ensure that the Default TOC is still **open**.

2. Edit book names.

   ☐ right-click the **Drugs_and_Alcohol** book and choose **Properties**

   ☐ remove the underscore from between the words

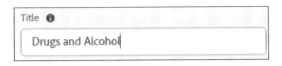

   ☐ click the **Apply** button

3. Reorder some of the pages in the TOC.

   ☐ open the **General_Office_Information** book

   ☐ select the **About This Guide** page

   ☐ from the top of the RoboHelp window, click the **Move Up** icon  repeatedly until the page is the first one listed in the **General_Office_Information** book

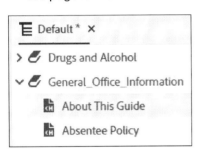

   Note: TOC Pages are not necessarily listed alphabetically. Instead, pages should be named and structured in a logical, meaningful way that best meets the needs of your users.

Book Structure Confidence Check

1. Move the **About This Guide** page above the books.

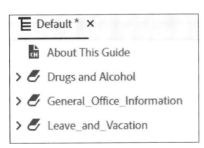

2. Rename the remaining book titles (remove the underscores).

3. Change the order of a few of the pages in the books as you see fit.

4. Save the project.

Style Sheets

A typical project contains hundreds, if not thousands, of topics. For the sake of simplicity, let's assume you have 500 topics. Each of those topics is going to contain one main heading. Several of the topics are likely to contain multiple subheadings. There's going to be normal body copy in every topic. Let's see, 500 main headings, hundreds of subheads, and thousands of normal paragraphs. You will likely want each of those 500 headings to have a consistent look. Perhaps you've decided upon Verdana, Bold, 14 points, and Centered alignment. That's as many as four commands per heading, multiplied by 500. Although Kevin isn't very good at multiplication, even he can figure out that it's going to take 2,000 steps to format all of the headings. Keep in mind that you have not even started formatting any of the remaining text. Tired yet? And don't get me started on how much work it's going to take to update the appearance of the text that you've just spent so much time formatting. I wouldn't want to do all of that work, and I'm betting that you wouldn't want to either.

Cascading Style Sheets (CSS) take the drudgery, and the work, out of formatting and updating the look of your topics. CSS files can contain dozens of styles that in turn can contain hundreds upon hundreds of formatting commands that you can assign to any topic. The beauty of a Style Sheet is that once you have assigned a Style Sheet to a topic, you can edit the style, which will in turn effect hundreds of changes in your project in minutes.

Guided Activity 21: Attach a Style Sheet to a Topic

1. Ensure that you are still working in the **project_structure_css** project from the **RoboHelpProjects > project_structure_css**.

2. Open a topic and display the paragraph markers.

   ❑ double-click the **About This Guide** topic to open the topic for editing

   ❑ choose **View > Show > Paragraph Markers**

   You should now be able to see the "hidden" paragraph markers in the topic.

   > About This Guide¶
   >
   > This guide has been prepared to assist Super Simplistic Solu
   > Solutions and its present policies and procedures.¶
   >
   > These policies and procedures are reviewed annually and re
   > immediaetly communicated to all employees.¶

   Notice the appearance of the topic text. You are about to change the appearance of the text in this topic and then all of your topics in the project.

3. Apply a style to a single topic.

   ❑ from within the open topic, right-click the middle of the text and choose **Topic Properties**

   The Properties area expands at the right of the RoboHelp window. There are three tabs: General, Styles, and Topic.

   ❑ select the **Topic** tab

   ❑ expand **Style Sheets**

❑ click the **Style Sheets** drop-down menu

The Style Sheets you see in the menu were either created automatically when the project was created (default.css) or created when Word documents were imported into the project (vacation.css for instance). All of the css files are stored in the Contents area within the **assets** folder.

❑ select **default.css** from the menu

Notice two things. First, the applied Style Sheet is listed below the Style Sheet menu. Second, the appearance of **About This Guide** topic text changes dramatically to reflect the current attributes of the default.css Style Sheet.

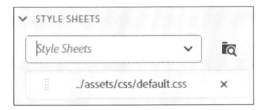

About This Guide¶
This guide has been prepared to assist Super Simplistic Solutions staf
Simplistic Solutions and its present policies and procedures.¶
These policies and procedures are reviewed annually and revised as r
the guide will be immediaetly communicated to all employees.¶
Nothing in this guide or any other document that is not specifically des
expressed or implied employment contract between the employee and
Solutions is strictly "at will" and terminable by either the employee or S
change in this policy can only be made by a written statement signed b

Note: You can click the **x** next to the Style Sheet name to remove the Style Sheet from the topic and return it to its previous formatting.

Guided Activity 22: Apply Paragraph Styles

1. Ensure that you are still working in the **project_structure_css** project.

2. Apply the Heading 1 paragraph style to a paragraph.

   ☐ in the **About This Guide** topic, click in the topic's first line of text (**About This Guide**)

   ☐ from the Properties panel at the right, click the **Styles** tab

   ☐ from the list of styles, click **Heading 1**

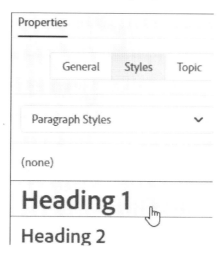

The first paragraph in the topic is formatted as Arial, Bold, 24 point, and white space has been added below the paragraph.

About This Guide¶

This guide has been prepared to assist Super Simplistic Solutions s
Simplistic Solutions and its present policies and procedures.¶
These policies and procedures are reviewed annually and revised a
the guide will be immediaetly communicated to all employees.¶
Nothing in this guide or any other document that is not specifically c
expressed or implied employment contract between the employee a
Solutions is strictly "at will" and terminable by either the employee c

3. Assign a Style Sheet to a topic and paragraph Style to topic text.

   ☐ from the **General Office Information** folder, open the **Overtime Policy** topic

   Notice that the **Styles** list in the Properties panel has no paragraph styles because you have not yet applied a Style Sheet to the topic.

   ☐ from the **Properties** panel, select the **Topic** tab

   ☐ from the **Style Sheet** drop-down menu, choose **default.css**

   ☐ click within the topic's main heading at the top of the page (within the phrase **Overtime Policy**)

   ☐ select the **Styles** tab and then select **Heading 1**

Styles Confidence Check

1. Open each topic in the project and assign the **Default** Style Sheet.

2. Assign the **Heading 1** style to the paragraph in each topic as necessary.

3. Open the **Termination Policy** topic and assign the **Heading 2** style to the following paragraphs:

   ❏ Resignation

   ❏ Disciplinary Policies and Procedures

   ❏ Unemployment Insurance

4. In the **Special Benefits** topic, assign the Heading 2 style to the following paragraphs:

   ❏ 401(k) Plan

   ❏ Workers Compensation Insurance

   ❏ Employee Assistance Program

5. In the **Electronic Communications Policy** topic, remove the extra paragraph breaks.

6. Save the project.

Custom Style Sheets

You can create your own Style Sheets and define your own paragraph styles complete with specific fonts, sizes, colors, spacing, and much more. The Style Sheet you create is an external file and can be imported into other RoboHelp projects and edited within RoboHelp or using a text editor (such as Notepad).

Font Usage

Although there are literally thousands of fonts you can use in your Help System, there are only **two** main font categories: *serif* (fonts with feet) and *sans serif* (fonts without feet). Two popular fonts are Times New Roman (serif) and Arial (sans serif). Below is an example of each.

This is an example of Times New Roman, a serif font.
This is an example of Arial, a sans-serif font.

Fonts are measured in points (dots) or pixels (squares). There are 72 points to an inch. Although both of the examples above are 14 points, the Arial example looks larger. Fonts like Arial are easy to read and are available on most devices. Because your Help System will usually be viewed via a computer or mobile device, it's a good idea to stick with common, readable fonts (like Arial or Verdana). You can find out more about fonts at **https://www.w3schools.com/csSref/ css_websafe_fonts.asp**.

Guided Activity 23: Create a Style Sheet

1. Ensure that you are still working in the **project_structure_css** project.

2. Create a style sheet.

   ☐ from **Contents**, expand the **assets** folder

   ☐ select the **CSS** folder and then click the **Options** icon

   ☐ choose **New > New Stylesheet**

   The New Stylesheet dialog box opens.

   ☐ name the style sheet **policies**

   ☐ click the **Done** button

   The style sheet has been added to the **css** folder.

3. Add a paragraph style to the policies style sheet.

☐ from within the **css** folder, double-click **policies.css**

☐ select **Paragraph Styles**

☐ notice that's there's a small toolbar above the CSS window

☐ click the **New Style** icon

The Add Style dialog box opens.

☐ from the tag list, scroll down and select the **p** tag (if necessary)

The **p** tag is used to control the appearance of paragraph text.

☐ click the **Done** button

4. Set the font properties for the paragraph style.

☐ expand the **Font** category

☐ from the first drop-down menu beneath **Font**, choose **Verdana**

☐ from the **Font Size** area, change the Font Size to **10 pt**

Note: The default unit of measurement is pixels (px). You'll need to type **pt** for points.

5. Change the paragraph spacing used in the paragraph style.

❏ expand the **Layout** category

❏ from the **Margin** area, click "Same value" icon 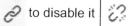 to disable it

❏ change the **Bottom Margin** to **12**

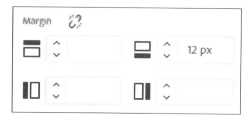

By disabling "Click to set same value for all sides," the Bottom Margin is the only margin that changes to 12. Had you not disabled the option, all of the margins would have changed to 12.

6. Add a heading 1 style to the policies style sheet.

❏ on the small toolbar above the CSS window, click the **New Style** icon

The Add Style dialog box reopens.

❏ from the tag list, scroll down and select **h1**

The h1 tag is used to control the appearance of the Heading 1 style.

❏ click the **Done** button

7. Set the font properties for the heading style.

   ❑ from the first drop-down menu beneath **Font**, choose **Verdana**

   ❑ change the Font Size to **14 pt**

8. Add paragraph spacing below the headings.

   ❑ if necessary, expand the **Layout** category

   ❑ from the **Margin** area, click "Same value" icon  to disable it

   ❑ change the **Bottom Margin** to **12**

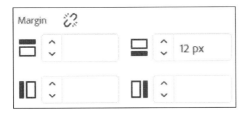

9. Save and close the **policies** style sheet.

NOTES

Adobe RoboHelp 2019: The Essentials (Second Edition)

Guided Activity 24: Remove and Apply a Topic's Style Sheet

1. Ensure that you are still working in the **project_structure_css** project.

2. Remove a style sheet.

   ☐ from the **General Office Information** folder, open the **Special Benefits** topic

   The topic is still using the default.css. Next, you'll remove the reference to the style sheet from the topic and apply your new policies style sheet.

   ☐ at the right of the RoboHelp window, select the **Topic** tab

   ☐ from the **Style Sheets** area, click the **Remove** icon next to the default.css reference

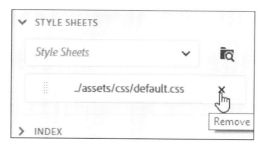

   ☐ click the **Yes** button to confirm the action

   The style sheet was not deleted from the project, just disconnected from the topic. Without the style sheet, the text in the Special Benefit topic doesn't look so good.

3. Attach a different style sheet to the topic.

   ☐ from the **Style Sheets** drop-down menu, choose **policies.css**

   The main heading and the body text take on the attributes of the h1 and p tags in the style sheet.

Edit Style Sheet Confidence Check

1. Open the **policies.css** file for editing.

2. Add an **h2** tag (this tag controls the second level headings).

3. Format the **h2** tag similarly to the **h1** tag (Verdana and **12 px** Bottom Margin), but set the Font Size to **11 pt**.

4. Save and close the style sheet.

   In the Special Benefits topic, the second level headings should all be formatted to match the h2 tag you just created.

5. Reopen the **policies.css** file.

6. Edit the **h1** tag, changing the **Font Color** to a **dark red**.

7. Save and close the style sheet.

   The color for the main heading should now be dark red.

Character Styles

When you format selected text (such as making a word bold and maroon), you are using a technique known as **inline formatting**. Have you ever used the Bold tool on selected text in programs like Microsoft Word or PowerPoint? Ever made text italic? If so, then you've applied an inline format. Using inline formatting is easy, but it can be a bad habit because inline formatting is as stubborn as a mule. If you attach a different Style Sheet to a topic, the inline formatting does not go away.

Imagine having to manually move through a project and changing every occurrence of text that is bold and maroon to italic and navy. That would be a tough task if there were just a few dozen such instances. But a few hundred? Ouch!

Much like Paragraph styles, Character styles allow you to quickly format selected text. Unlike Paragraph styles (such as the Heading styles you used earlier in this module), Character styles can be applied only to selected text. Once applied, Character styles are easy to update (just like Paragraph styles).

Guided Activity 25: Create and Apply a Character Style

1. Ensure that you are still working in the **project_structure_css** project.

2. Open the **policies** style sheet for editing.

3. Add a Character style.

   ☐ from the list of **Styles**, select **Character Styles**

   ☐ on the small toolbar above the CSS window, click the **New Style** icon

   The Add Style dialog box opens.

   ☐ in the tag field, type **.emphasis** after the word **span**

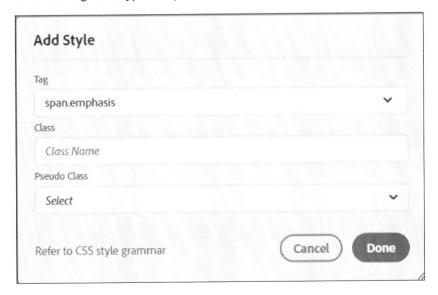

   ☐ click the **Done** button

   ☐ with the new **span.emphasis** tag selected, change the Font Color to **a dark red**

4. Save and close the style sheet.

5. Apply a Character Style to selected topic text.

   ☐ if necessary, open the **Special Benefits** topic

   ☐ in the first paragraph of the topic, highlight the phrase **21 years or older**

   ☐ at the right side of the RoboHelp window, select the **Styles** tab

   ☐ from the **Styles** drop-down menu, choose **All Styles**

   ☐ select the **emphasis** tag you just created

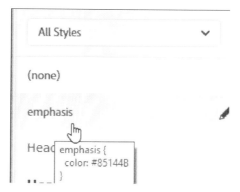

Only the selected text in the topic takes on the appearance of the emphasis tag. The selected text should now be maroon.

6. Save your work.

Character Style Confidence Check

1. In the **Employee Assistance Program** section, highlight the phrase **resolve your problems** in the second paragraph and apply the **emphasis** tag to the text.

2. Go through the entire project and remove the references to the **default**.css. In its place, apply **policies**.css. (If any topics are referencing other/multiple CSS files, remove those references.)

3. Open the **Termination Policy** topic and apply the **emphasis** tag to the following phrases:

   ☐ First Notice

   ☐ Second Notice

   ☐ Final Notice

   ☐ Discharge

4. Open the **policies.css** file for editing.

5. Change the color of the **span.emphasis** tag to **any color you like** (the tag is located in the **Character Styles** folder of the policies.css file).

   After closing and saving the style sheet, all instances of the emphasis tag (across any topics where you've applied it) should update to the new color.

6. Save the project.

List Styles

There are two main types of lists used in HTML (and in RoboHelp): numbered lists (or ordered lists) and bulleted lists (unordered lists). The formatting for both types of lists is controlled by styles that are part of a style sheet.

Guided Activity 26: Format a Bulleted List

1. Ensure that you are still working in the **Project Structure** project.

2. Open the **Pets in the Office Policy** topic for editing.

   During the last Confidence Check, you were instructed to apply the **policies** style sheet to all of the topics in the project. You may have noticed after doing so that the formatting of the bulleted list in the Pets policy did not update along with the rest of the topic. The reason? There isn't a style in the policies style sheet that instructs the topic how to format the list so the text uses the default formatting (for example, Times New Roman for font).

   A Few Simple Rules¶

   - Your pet bites, we bite you... and you pay the piper
   - Your pet poops in the office, you clean it up immediately
   - Just say NO to barking!!!!
   - Your pet must be on a leash at all times when NOT in your office
   - All pets, except Cats and Dogs, must always be in an approved cage or aquarium
   ---

3. Open the **policies** style sheet for editing.

4. Add a List Style for the bulleted list.

   ☐ select **List Styles**

   ☐ click the **New Style** icon ⊕

   By default, the tag that appears in the tag list is the **ol** tag. The **ol** tag controls the formatting of numbered lists. Although it's worth setting up the formatting for this tag, let's focus instead on the tag that controls bulleted lists.

   ☐ from the drop-down menu, choose the **ul** tag

   ☐ click the **Done** button

   ☐ from the **Apply Formatting** drop-down menu, choose **Bullets**

   > Apply Formatting to:
   > Bullets ⌄

   ☐ from the **Font** area, change the Font to **Verdana** and change the Font Size to **10 pt**

   ☐ from the **Apply Formatting** drop-down menu, choose **Content**

   > Apply Formatting to:
   > Content ⌄

   ☐ from the **Font** area, change the Font to **Verdana** and change the Font Size to **10 pt**

5. Save and close the style sheet.

In the Pets in the Office Policy topic, the bulleted list is automatically formatted to match the **ul** tag you just added.

A Few Simple Rules¶

- Your pet bites, we bite you... and you pay the piper
- Your pet poops in the office, you clean it up immediately
- Just say NO to barking!!!!
- Your pet must be on a leash at all times when NOT in your office
- All pets, except Cats and Dogs, must always be in an approved cage or aquarium

Banned From the Office!¶

- All snakes
- Rodents
- Spiders

List Style Confidence Check

1. Open the **policies** style sheet for editing.

2. Select the **ul** list style.

3. Change **Apply Formatting to** to **Bullets**.

4. Change the **style** of the bullets used in the bulleted list to **circle**.

```
Style
circle                                      ⌄
```

A Few Simple Rules¶

- Your pet bites, we bite you...
- Your pet poops in the office, y
- Just say NO to barking!!!!
- Your pet must be on a leash a
- All pets, except Cats and Dog

5. Change the **style** of the bullets used in the bulleted list to **square**.

6. Change the **style** of the bullets used in the bulleted list back to the original style: **discs**.

7. Save and close the project.

iCONLOGiC
"Skills and Drills" Learning

Module 4: Linking

In This Module You Will Learn About:

- Linking to External Content, page 54
- Hyperlinks, page 59
- Bookmarks, page 62
- Popup Links, page 65

And You Will Learn To:

- Link to a Word Document, page 54
- Insert Links, page 59
- Insert Bookmarks, page 62
- Insert Auto-Sizing Popups, page 65

Linking to External Content

You learned earlier how to import Word documents into your project (see page 28). After the import process, the original source document has little value because its contents have been copied into the RoboHelp project as topics. Any changes you make to the imported content from within RoboHelp will not appear in the original Word document; changes to the original Word document will not appear in RoboHelp. If changes have been made to the original Word document and you want those changes to appear in the RoboHelp project, you'll need to make the identical changes to the content within RoboHelp or delete the imported topic(s) from the RoboHelp project and re-import the updated Word content. Neither of these two scenarios is ideal.

If the Word content you need to import into your RoboHelp project is a "moving target" and is constantly being updated by an author or subject matter expert (SME), consider linking to the source document instead of importing.

Guided Activity 27: Link to a Word Document

1. Open a source document using Microsoft Word.

   ☐ start **Microsoft Word**

   ☐ from **RoboHelp2019Data > content**, use Word to open **Holiday Schedule.docx**

   This is a typical Word document. The first paragraph has been formatted using Word's heading style. The rest of the document is using Word's Normal style.

Super Simplistic Solutions Holiday Schedule
Super Simplistic Solutions celebrates the following holidays:

2019
January 1: New Year's Day
January 21: Martin Luther King Day
May 27: Memorial Day
July 4: Independence Day
September 2: Labor Day
October 14: Columbus Day
November 11: Veterans Day
November 28: Thanksgiving Day
December 25: Christmas Day!

2020
January 1: New Year's Day
January 20: Martin Luther King Day
February 18: Washington's Birthday
May 25: Memorial Day
July 4: Independence Day
September 7: Labor Day
October 12: Columbus Day
November 11: Veterans Day
November 26: Thanksgiving Day
December 25: Christmas Day

---

2. Close Microsoft Word.

3. Open an existing RoboHelp project.

    ☐ use RoboHelp, choose **File > Open Project**

    ☐ from the **RoboHelp2019Data** folder, open the **RoboHelpProjects** folder

    ☐ open the **linking** folder

    ☐ open **linking.rhpj**

4. Create a folder for linked content.

    ☐ from the **Contents** area, right-click below the **Leave and Vacation** folder and choose **New > New Folder**

    ☐ name the new folder **Linked_Docs**

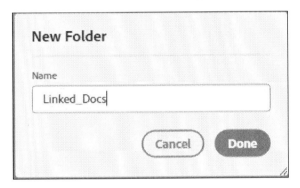

    ☐ click the **Done** button

5. Link to a Word document.

    ☐ right-click the **Linked_Docs** folder and choose **Link > Link File**

    ☐ from **RoboHelp2019Data > content** open **Holiday Schedule.docx**

The file appears in the Linked_Docs folder. Notice the green icon to the left of the file name. The green icon indicates that the document in RoboHelp and its source back in the **RoboHelp2019Data > content** folder are synchronized.

6. Create a topic from the linked Word document.

   ❑ right-click the linked document and choose **Create/Update Topics**

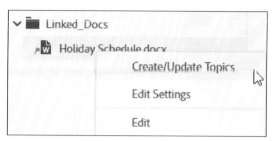

7. Explore the new topic.

   ❑ from the **Linked_Docs** folder, open the **Holiday Schedule** folder

   Notice that in addition to a new topic, the process of creating topics from the Word documents has also created a style sheet (css) file.

   ❑ open the **Holiday Schedule** topic

   Notice that the content in the RoboHelp topic matches the content in the linked Word document.

8. Close the topic.

9. Edit the source document.

   ❑ start **Microsoft Word**

   ❑ from **RoboHelp2019Data > content**, use Word to open **Holiday Schedule.docx**

   ❑ delete all of the **2019** dates

   ❑ from the **2023** section, change **2023** to **2022**

10. Save and close the Word document and return to the RoboHelp project.

11. In the **Holiday Schedule** folder, notice that the reference to the source Word document is **red**, an indication that the content in your project is not in sync with the source document.

12. Sync the topic content in RoboHelp with the linked Word document.

☐ from the **Linked_Docs** folder, right-click **Holiday Schedule.docx**

☐ choose **Sync > From Source to Project**

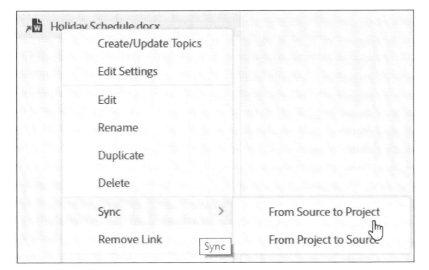

The icon color to the left of the Word document reference is once again green.

☐ right-click the linked document and choose **Create/Update Topics**

13. Explore the updated topic.

☐ from the **Linked_Docs** folder, open the **Holiday Schedule** folder

☐ open the **Holiday Schedule** topic

Notice that the changes made to the topic in Word appear in the RoboHelp topic.

14. Close the topic.

External Content Links Confidence Check

1. Using **Microsoft Word**, reopen the **Holiday Schedule** document.

2. Apply **bullets** to all of the vacation dates.

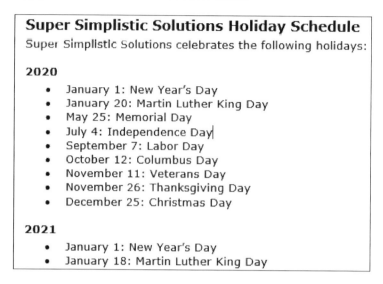

Super Simplistic Solutions Holiday Schedule

Super Simplistic Solutions celebrates the following holidays:

2020
- January 1: New Year's Day
- January 20: Martin Luther King Day
- May 25: Memorial Day
- July 4: Independence Day
- September 7: Labor Day
- October 12: Columbus Day
- November 11: Veterans Day
- November 26: Thanksgiving Day
- December 25: Christmas Day

2021
- January 1: New Year's Day
- January 18: Martin Luther King Day

3. Save the document and then exit Microsoft Word.

4. Back in RoboHelp, **Sync** Holiday Schedule.docx to the Source document.

5. Update the Topics.

6. In RoboHelp, open the **Holiday Schedule** topic. Notice that although your changes have been applied, the topic is not using the same style sheet as the other topics in your project.

7. From the **Properties** area, **Topic** tab, **remove** Holiday Schedule.css.

8. Apply **policies.css** to the **Holiday Schedule** topic.

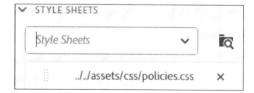

9. Close the topic.

Note: Because the **Holiday Schedule** topic is linked to a Word document, should you Sync to the Source document again any changes made to the topic from within RoboHelp will be lost (for instance, the Holiday Schedule.css will once again replace policies.css).

Hyperlinks

Hyperlinks allow your users to jump from one project location to another. There are several types of hyperlinks you can create including standard links (links that typically jump from one Help topic to another), web address links (links that open a website or resource), email links (links that send an email to a recipient you specify), and links to local files.

Guided Activity 28: Insert Links

1. Ensure that the **linking** project is still open.

2. From the **Drugs and Alcohol** folder, open the **Drug Policy** topic.

3. Add text to a topic.

   ☐ in the second paragraph ("If you are having difficulties resulting..."), click after the word **drug**

   ☐ press [**spacebar**] and then type **or alcohol**

   The sentence should now read "If you are having difficulties resulting from drug or alcohol use, Super Simplistic Solutions may request that you enter a rehabilitation program."

4. Insert a hyperlink to another topic in the project.

   ☐ double-click the word **alcohol** that you just typed (to highlight the word)

   ☐ from the top of the RoboHelp window, click the **Insert Link** icon

   The **Link to** dialog box opens.

   ☐ from the **Link to** area, ensure that **Project Files** is selected

   ☐ from the **Drugs and Alcohol** folder, select **Alcohol Policy**

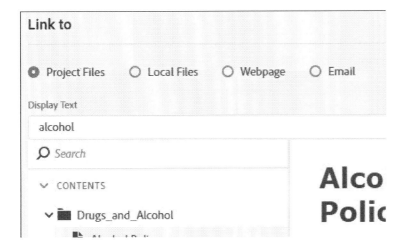

   ☐ click the **Link** button

   Now that you have made the word "alcohol" a hyperlink, the text takes on the traditional appearance of linked text (**blue** with an **underline**).

5. Insert a link in another topic by dragging and dropping.

   ❏ open the **Alcohol Policy** topic

   ❏ at the end of the topic text, click after the last word and press [**enter**] to add a new paragraph

   ❏ type **See also:**

   ❏ from the **Contents** area, drag the **Drug policy** topic to the right of the **See also** text that you just typed

   > 📁 assets
   > ∨ 📁 Drugs_and_Alcohol
   >   📄 Alcohol Policy
   >   📄 Drug Policy   •••
   > ∨ 📁 General_Office_Informa...n
   >   📄 Absentee Policy
   >   📄 Conflict Resolution Policy
   >   📄 Electronic Communications
   >   📄 Mission Statement
   >   📄 Nondiscrimination Policy

   body ▸ div ▸ p

   # Alcohol

   Super Simplistic Sc
   employee's assigne

   Such action will sul
   assistance to an en

   If your work perfor
   help for your condi

   See als...

   If your work performance indicates you
   help for your condition or recurrence of

   See also: Drug Policy

   Your project now has two hyperlinks to existing topics.

6. Save the project.

7. Preview a topic and test the hyperlinks.

   ❏ ensure that the Alcohol Policy topic is still open

   ❏ at the far right of the RoboHelp window, click the **Preview** icon 🔍

   Notice that the editing tools at the top of the topic window disappear.

   ❏ click the **Drug Policy** link

   The Drug Policy topic opens in its own window.

   ❏ click the word **alcohol** in the open Drug Policy window

   You should be sent to the Alcohol Policy topic.

8. Close the preview window and then click the **Author** icon ✏️ to leave Preview mode.

Links Confidence Check

1. Open the **Payroll Policy** topic.

2. Add the following new paragraph at the end of the topic:
   See also: Overtime Policy.

3. Highlight the phrase **Overtime Policy** and link the text to the **Overtime Policy** topic.

4. Open the **Overtime Policy** topic and add the following new paragraph at the end of the topic: **See also: Payroll Policy**.

5. Link the phrase **Payroll Policy** to the Payroll Policy topic.

   Note: You can remove an unwanted link by right-clicking any link and choosing **Remove Hyperlink.**

6. Open the **Payroll Policy** topic.

7. Click after the hyperlink to **Overtime Policy** and press [**spacebar**].

8. Type **or Vacation Policy**.

9. Hyperlink the words **Vacation Policy** to the **Vacation Policy** topic.

10. Save the project.

11. Preview the topics and test your new links.

12. Close the Preview window.

13. Open the **Drug Policy** Topic.

14. Notice that there's a misspelled word in the last paragraph ("ditribute").

15. Right-click the word and replace it with **distribute**.

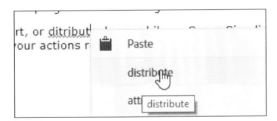

Note: RoboHelp allows you correct spelling errors on the fly as you've just demonstrated. You can also run a traditional Spell Check by choosing **Edit > Spell Check**. You can Spell Check a single topic, all topics, or All Project Files. While choosing All Project Files takes longer, I would suggest you go with this option at least once every so often so that you can ensure you've checked for spelling errors within the TOC, Index, and all topics.

Bookmarks

You can use bookmarks to create links to specific locations within a topic. For instance, you can create a bookmark in the middle of a large topic. You can create a link in a topic that jumps a user into the large topic and to the location you specify when you insert the bookmark. You can link to a bookmark from any other topic in your project, from an Index keyword, or a TOC entry.

Guided Activity 29: Insert Bookmarks

1. Ensure that the **linking** project is still open.

2. From the **General Office Information** folder, open the **Termination Policy** topic.

3. Insert a Bookmark.

   ☐ at the top of the topic, click to the left of the **Resignation** heading

   ☐ from the toolbar above the topic, click the **Insert Bookmark** icon

   The Bookmark dialog box opens.

   ☐ in the **ID** field, replace the placeholder text with **resignation**

   Bookmark

   ID:

resignation

   Bookmarks in this topic:

ID	PARAGRAPH

   ☐ click the **Insert** button

   A bookmark icon appears to the left of the word Resignation. This is a visual indicator that a bookmark has been inserted.

   ## Terminatio

   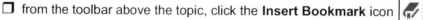

   Resignation¶

   If you voluntarily terminate y
   The company requires a mini

Bookmarks Confidence Check

1. Insert a second bookmark to the left of the second heading (**Disciplinary Policies and Procedures**) with the ID **disciplinary_policies_and_procedures**.

2. Add a third bookmark for the last heading in the topic with the ID **unemployment_insurance**.

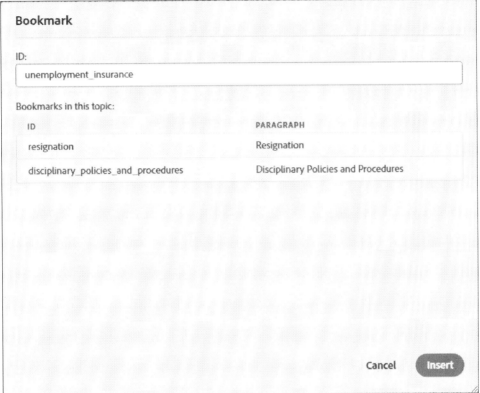

Bookmark

ID:

unemployment_insurance

Bookmarks in this topic:

ID	PARAGRAPH
resignation	Resignation
disciplinary_policies_and_procedures	Disciplinary Policies and Procedures

Cancel   Insert

3. Still in the Termination Policy topic, click after the main heading (**Termination Policy**) and press [**enter**] to add a line between the main heading and subheading **Resignation**.

4. Type **Our Termination Policy consists of three main areas: Resignation, Disciplinary Policies and Procedures and Unemployment Insurance.**

Termination Policy¶

Our Termination Policy consists of three main areas: Resignation, Disciplinary Policies and Procedures and Unemployment Insurance.¶

¶Resignation¶

If you voluntarily terminate your employment with Super Simplistic Solutions, you are required to provide a written statement of resi The company requires a minimum of 2 weeks' notice.¶

You will be required to turn in to the Human Resources Director your Policy and Procedures Manual and your building security cards, I

5. Save the project.

6. Highlight the word **Resignation** in the text that you just typed.

7. Display the **Link to** dialog box.

8. From the **General Office Information Book**, expand the **Termination Policy** topic to see the bookmarks you added.

9. Select the **resignation** bookmark and then click the **Link** button.

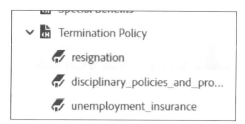

10. Link the text **Disciplinary Policies and Procedures** and **Unemployment Insurance** to their respective bookmarks.

11. **Preview** the topic. 🔍

12. Test the bookmarks (by clicking any of the links at the top of the page).

13. When finished, return to **Author** mode. ✏️

14. In the **Contents** area, right-click beneath the last folder and create a new folder named **Corporate_Officers**.

15. Create a new topic in the **Corporate_Officers** folder and name it **Our President**.

16. Add the following text to the new topic: **The president of Super Simplistic Solutions is Biff Bifferson. Our tireless leader can be reached by dialing extension 123 or by sending an Email.**

Our President¶

The president of Super Simplistic Solutions is Biff Bifferson. Our tireless leader can be reached by dialing extension 123 or by sending an Email.¶

---

17. On the Properties panel, remove the reference to **default.css** from the **Our President** topic.

18. Apply **policies.css** style sheet to the **Our President** topic.

19. Save the project.

Popup Links

The hyperlinks you have added to topics have taken users from one topic to another. If you want users to link to a small window within a topic, popups are just the ticket. When users click the hyperlink, the content they link to can appear in either an auto-sizing popup (which is only as big as necessary to display the content) or a custom-sized popup (which appears in a window size that you control).

Guided Activity 30: Insert Auto-Sizing Popups

1. Ensure that the **linking** project is still open and that you have created the **Our President** topic (per the Confidence Check on the previous page).

2. Insert an auto-sizing popup.

   ☐ open the **About This Guide** topic

   ☐ highlight the word **president** (the last word in the topic)

   ☐ from the top of the RoboHelp window, click the **Insert Link** icon 🔗

   The **Link to** dialog box opens.

   ☐ from the Contents area, open the **Corporate Officers** folder

   ☐ select the **Our President** topic (you created both the folder and topic during the last activity)

   ☐ from the **Display In** area, select **Auto-sized popup**

   Display In
   ○ Frame   ● Auto-sized popup   ○ Custom-sized popup

   ☐ click the **Link** button

3. Preview the **About This Guide** topic and test the pop-up link by clicking the link to the **president** topic.

   t specifically designed as an "employment contract" const
   e employee and Super Simplistic Solutions . Employment
   ee or Super Simplistic Solutions at any time with or witho
   by the president.

   # Our President

   The president of Super Simplistic Solution:
   Bifferson. Our tireless leader can be reach
   extension 123 or by sending an Email.

4. Return to **Author** mode and then **save** the project.

Popup Hyperlink Confidence Check

1. Open the **Our President** topic and select the word **Email** that you typed.

2. Insert a hyperlink and, from the **Link to** area, choose **Email**.

3. In the **Address** field, type **biff.bifferson@supersimplisticsolutions.com** (click the Link button when finished to close the Link to dialog box).

> ## Link to
>
> ○ Project Files   ○ Local Files   ○ Webpage   ● Email
>
> Display Text
>
> Email
>
> Address
>
> biffbiff@supersimplisticsolutions.com

When clicked by your users, the Email link starts the user's email application and addresses the email to **biff.bifferson@supersimplisticsolutions.com**.

4. Create a new topic in the **Corporate_Officers** folder called **Human Resources**.

5. Add the following text to the new topic: **Our Human Resources Director is Brandy McNeill at extension 552.**

6. Create a new topic in the **Corporate_Officers** folder called **Information Services Director**.

7. Add the following text to the new topic: **Our Information Services Director is Travis DonBullian at extension 33.**

8. Create a new topic in the **Corporate_Officers** folder called **Webmaster**.

9. Add the following text to the new topic: **Our Webmaster is Sandra Stimson. She can be reached at extension 34.**

10. Open the **Overtime Policy** topic.

11. Highlight the words **Human Resources** (in the "Authorization for Employees' Earned Compensatory Time" paragraph near the end of the topic).

12. Link the phrase to the **Human Resources** topic in an **Auto-sized popup**.

13. Open the **Electronic Communications Policy** topic.

14. Add a blank paragraph at the end of the topic.

15. Type **See also: Information Services Director or Our Webmaster**.

16. Insert Auto-sized popup links for the phrases **Information Services Director** and **Our Webmaster** that link to the appropriate topics.

17. Save and close the project.

iCONLOGiC

"Skills and Drills" Learning

Module 5: Images and Multimedia

In This Module You Will Learn About:

And You Will Learn To:

Images

Given today's distractions and stress levels, people who use your Help System want to quickly find information. Unlike the old days, Help Systems cannot survive on text alone. A more modern approach to Help Authoring is to go with a minimal amount of text and use helpful, visually-appealing images.

RoboHelp allows you to import such image formats as **GIFs, JPEGs, BMPs, ICOs, SVGs**, and **PNGs** with the most common being GIFs, JPEGs, and PNGs. You can learn about the strengths and weakness of each image format at https://www.w3.org/Graphics/.

Guided Activity 31: Insert an Image

1. Open the **images_multimedia** RoboHelp project. (The project is located within **RoboHelp2019Data > RoboHelpProjects**.)

2. Display the Topic List panel and add a column.

   ☐ choose **View >Topic List**

   All of the topics in the project appear on a single screen.

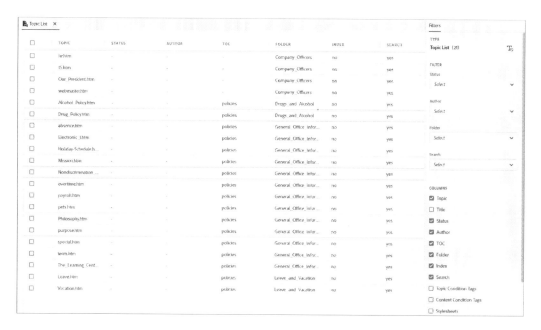

Although the list of topics includes topic file names, TOC assignment, and more, it's likely that topic titles aren't displayed. You'll add the titles next.

☐ from the far right of the RoboHelp window, within the **Columns** area, click **Title**

In the Topic List, notice that you can see all of the topic Titles. (The remaining columns can be left on or off at this point.)

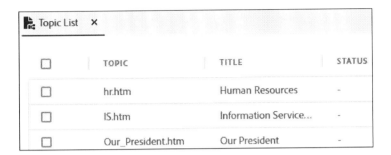

3. Use the Topic List to open a topic.

   ☐ from within the **Topic List**, right-click the **Mission Statement** topic and choose **Edit**

4. Insert an image.

   ☐ from within the **Mission Statement** topic, click at the end of the topic and press [**enter**] to insert a blank line

Our Mission

To continually create solutions for all of the world's problems. Those solutions r super... yet simplistic.

   ☐ from above the topic, click the **Insert Image** icon

The Insert Image dialog box opens.

   ☐ select **Local Files**
   ☐ click the **Browse** icon
   ☐ from the **RoboHelp2019Data** folder, open the **images** folder
   ☐ open the **puzzle.jpg** image file

A preview of the image appears in the Preview area.

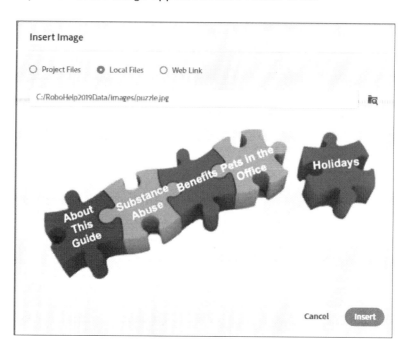

☐ click the **Insert** button

The image appears in the topic at the exact location of the insertion point.

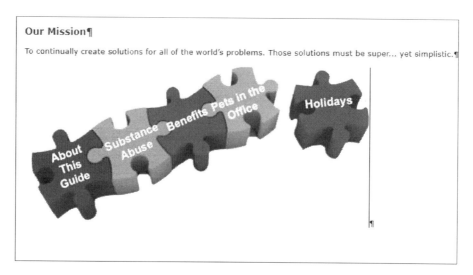

5. Save the project.

    Note: If you want to use an imported image in another topic, you do not need to import it a second time. Instead, go to **Contents > assets > images** and drag the image into any topic.

Guided Activity 32: Add Alternate Text and an Image Title

1. Ensure that you're still working in the images_multimedia project.

2. Add Alternate Text to an image.

    ☐ still working in the **Mission Statement** topic, select the puzzle image you just inserted

    ☐ from the **Properties** panel at the right, select the **General** tab

    ☐ click in the **Alternate Text** area and type **Image containing links to popular topics.**

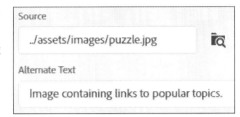

The Alternate Text appears in published output if the image cannot be displayed. This happens when accessibility devices read your content out loud for visually impaired users. Typically, Alternate Text is a brief description of the image.

3. Add an Image Title.

    ☐ still working in the Properties panel, click in the **Image Title** area and type **Image Map: Links to Popular Topics**

The Image Title appears in published output when the user hovers the cursor over the image.

4. Preview the topic.

5. Test the Image Title by moving your mouse over the puzzle image.

    The Image Title appears as your mouse hovers over the puzzle image.

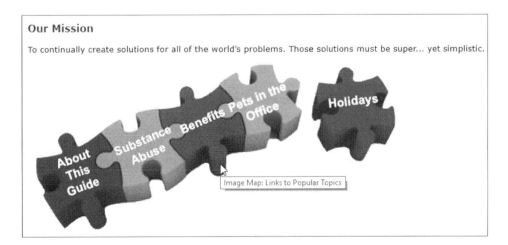

6. Return to Author mode.

7. Save the project.

Images Confidence Check

1. Open the **Our President** topic and click to the left of the text "The president of Super Simplistic Solutions is Biff Bifferson."

2. From **RoboHelp2019Data > images**, insert the **biff_baby.jpg** image.

3. Edit the Properties of the graphic you just inserted:

   ☐ Add the following Alternate Text: **Image of Biff Bifferson.**

   ☐ Add the following Image Title: **Our President, Biff Bifferson**

   ☐ Change the **Width** to **64** and press [**tab**] or [**enter**].

   Because **Maintain Aspect Ratio** 🔒 is enabled by default, notice that the image's **Height** automatically changes to **91** (ensuring that the image is resized proportionally).

4. Change the **Text wrapping** to **Right**.

   Text wrapping will move the image to the right side of the screen and force the text to wrap around it. Depending upon how large your RoboHelp window is, you'll see the text wrapping without having to preview the topic.

   Our President¶

   The president of Super Simplistic Solutions is Biff Bifferson. Our tireless leader can be reached by dialing extension 123 or by sending an Email to him.¶

   ---

5. Open the **Webmaster** topic.

6. Click to the left of the text "Our Webmaster is Sandra Stimson" and insert the following image: **sandra_baby.jpg**.

7. Edit the Properties for the image.

   ☐ Add the following **Image Title** and **Alternate Text** to the image: **Our Webmaster, Sandra Stimson**.

   ☐ Change the Width of the image to **116**.

❏ Change its **Text wrapping** to **Right**.

Webmaster¶

Our Webmaster is Sandra Stimson. She can be reached at extension 34.¶

8. Open the **Human Resources** topic.

9. Click to the left of the text "Our Human Resources Director is Brandy McNeill at extension 552" and insert the following image: **brandy_baby.jpg**.

10. Edit the image Properties:

❏ Add the following **Image Title** and **Alternate Text**: **Our HR Director, Brandy McNeill.**

❏ Change its **Width** to **120**.

❏ Change its **Text wrapping** to **Right**.

Human Resources¶

Our Human Resources Director is Brandy McNeill at extension 552.¶

11. Open the **Information Services Director** topic.

12. Click to the left of the text "Our Information Services Director is Travis DonBullian at extension 33" and insert the following image: **travis_baby.jpg**.

13. Edit the image Properties:

❏ Add the following **Image Title** and **Alternate Text** to the image: **Travis and his big sister, Matilda.**

❏ Change its **Width** to **73**.

❏ Change its **Text wrapping** to **Right**.

Information Services Director¶

Our Information Services Director is Travis DonBullian at extension 33.¶

14. Save the project.

Image Maps

Image Maps allow the user to click on a particular area (hotspot) of an image and jump to a different area of a Help System. Image Maps are made up of two elements: an image and multiple hotspots. Hotspots (also known as clickable regions) can target websites, topics, bookmarks, email addresses, or files. You can create circle, polygon, or rectangle clickable regions.

Guided Activity 33: Add Hotspots to a Graphic

1. Ensure that the **images_multimedia** project is still open.

2. Insert an image within a topic to be used as the image map.

   ❑ open the **Mission Statement** topic

   ❑ click at the end of the text **yet simplistic.**

   ❑ press [**enter**] to create a new paragraph

   ❑ type **Use the image below to move around this Help System.**

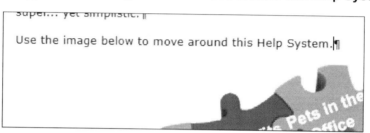

3. Insert an image map on the puzzle image.

   ❑ right-click the **puzzle** graphic and choose **Insert Image Map**

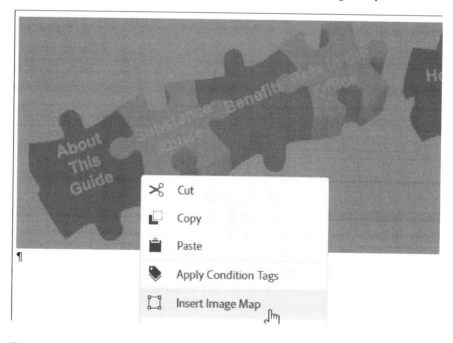

The Image Map dialog box opens.

4. Add a hotspot to the image map.

   ☐ select the **Insert Rectangle** icon

   ☐ draw a rectangle over the words **About This Guide**

A red box (a hotspot) surrounds the **About This Guide** area of the image map. You can move the red box, resize it, or delete it (using the Trash icon). Next, you'll link the hotspot to an existing topic.

5. Link a hotspot to a topic.

   ☐ double-click the rectangle hotspot

   The **Link to** dialog box opens.

   ☐ ensure **Project Files** is selected

   ☐ from the **General Office Information** folder, select **About This Guide**

   ☐ click the **Link** button

   Although nothing appears to change, when you hover your mouse over the hotspot, a popup lets you know that you've linked the hotspot to the About This Guide topic (purpose.htm).

Image Map Confidence Check

NOTES

1. Insert a rectangular hotspot that links the words **Substance Abuse** on the image map to the **Drug Policy** topic.

   Note: If you accidentally select the wrong target topic, double-click the hotspot and select a different topic.

2. Create a hotspot for **Benefits** that links to the **Special Benefits** topic.

3. Create a hotspot for **Pets in the Office** that links to the **Pets in the Office** topic.

4. Create a hotspot for **Holidays** that links to the **Holiday Schedule** topic.

5. When finished, click the **Done** button.

6. Preview the Mission Statement topic and test the image map links.

   When you click any of the blocks in the image map, the topic you targeted for each hotspot opens.

7. Close the topic's preview window.

8. Return to **Author** mode.

9. Save the project.

eLearning Integration

If you have created eLearning courses using tools such as Adobe Captivate, TechSmith Camtasia, or Articulate Storyline, you can import published content into RoboHelp. During the lessons that follow, you will import Adobe Captivate Demos into a project and then insert the imported interactive eLearning content into a topic.

Guided Activity 34: Import Captivate Demos into a Project

1. Ensure that the **images_multimedia** project is still open.

2. Create a folder for the eLearning content.

   ☐ right-click beneath the last folder in the **Contents** area and choose **New > New Folder**

   ☐ name the new folder **eLearning**

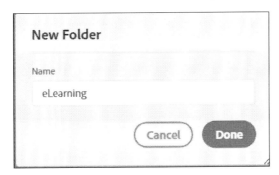

   ☐ click the **Done** button

3. Import an Adobe Captivate Demo.

   ☐ right-click the **eLearning** folder and choose **Import > Adobe Captivate Demo**

   ☐ navigate to **RoboHelp2019Data > eLearning**

   ☐ open the **StartAnApplication** folder

   ☐ open **index.html**

4. Import a second Adobe Captivate Demo.

   ☐ right-click the **eLearning** folder and choose **Import > Adobe Captivate Demo**

   ☐ from the **eLearning** folder, open the **SaveFile** folder

   ☐ open **index.html**

5. Import a third and final Adobe Captivate Demo.

   ☐ right-click the **eLearning** folder and choose **Import > Adobe Captivate Demo**

   ☐ from the **eLearning** folder, open the **CopyPasteBetweenApps** folder

   ☐ open **index.html**

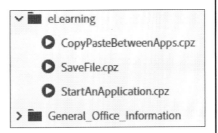

Guided Activity 35: Insert Captivate Demos into Topics

1. Ensure that the **images_multimedia** project is still open.

2. Insert an Adobe Captivate demo into a topic.

   ☐ from the **General Office Information** folder, open the **The Learning Center** topic

   ☐ click after the **Start an Application** heading and press [**enter**] to add a blank line

   ☐ from the toolbar above the topic, click the **Insert Multimedia** icon ▐◼ and choose **Adobe Captivate Demo** from the drop-down menu

   The Adobe Captivate Demo dialog box opens.

   ☐ from the **eLearning** folder, select **StartAnApplication**

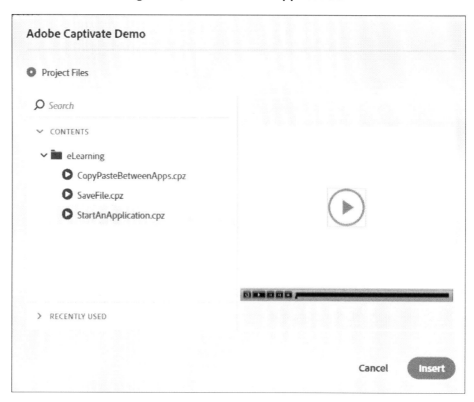

   ☐ click the **Insert** button

   A placeholder for the Captivate Demo appears. Next, you'll resize the placeholder so that it's the same size as the Captivate Demo (the imported demo is 640 x 480 pixels).

3. Resize a Captivate Demo.

   ☐ with the video placeholder selected, go to the **Properties** panel, **General** tab

   ☐ from the **Width** and **Height** area, disable **Maintain Aspect Ratio** 🔓 by clicking the lock icon

   ☐ change the Width of the demo to **640** and the Height to **480**

eLearning Confidence Check

1. Still working within The Learning Center topic, add a paragraph after the **Save a File** subhead.

2. Insert the **SaveFile** Adobe Captivate Demo.

3. Add a paragraph after the **Copy and Paste Content Between Applications** subhead.

4. Insert the **CopyPasteBetweenApps** Adobe Captivate Demo.

5. Resize both demos to **640 x 480**.

6. Save the project.

7. Preview **The Learning Center** topic and interact with the Adobe Captivate Demos.

8. Return to Author mode.

Drop-down Text

Using RoboHelp's Drop-down Text feature, you can quickly take a long, overwhelming topic and make it manageable for your users. For instance, consider The Learning Center topic. The topic contains three interactive eLearning lessons that appear on the screen at the same time. There is so much going on within the topic, users are likely to become overpowered by the content. Using Drop-down Text, you can effectively hide the simulations within each of the three subheads. As users click the appropriate subhead, the eLearning lesson appears.

Guided Activity 36: Create Drop-Down Text

1. Ensure that the **images_multimedia** project is still open.

2. If necessary, open the **The Learning Center** topic and that you're in Author mode.

3. Insert Drop-down Text.

    ❏ right-click the first demo (Start an Application) and choose **Cut**

    The video has not been deleted. Instead, it's hanging out on the clipboard. You'll paste it back within the topic shortly.

    ❏ highlight the **Start an Application** heading

    ❏ on the toolbar above the topic, click the **Create Drop-down Text** icon

    Placeholder text appears beneath the heading ("Type your drop-down text here.").

    ❏ highlight the placeholder text and **paste** the demo on the clipboard in place of the text

    The selected heading text becomes a link with the demo beneath.

4. Test the Drop-Down Text.

    ❏ preview the topic

    Notice that your first Captivate demo is not currently visible.

    ❏ click the **Start an Application** heading

    The demo appears.

    ❏ click the **Start an Application** heading again

    The demo disappears and the topic gets shorter. How slick is that? Using this effect, you can quickly make some of your longer topics more manageable for users.

    ❏ return to **Author** mode

Drop-Down Text and Images Confidence Check

1. Use Drop-Down Text for the other two headings and demos

2. Preview the topic and test the Drop-Down Text links.

3. When finished, return to Author mode.

4. Open the **Pets in the Office Policy** topic.

5. Insert the **dog.gif** image into the topic (in front of the phrase "Pets... we love them."

6. Change the **Text wrapping** of the dog image to **Right**.

7. Change the **Width** of the dog image to **150**.

8. Add the following **Alternate Text** and **Title** to the dog image: **Dogs are allowed in the office.**

9. From the **Properties** panel, **Layout** section, locate the **Padding** area.

   Padding allows you to add space between the image and nearby text.

10. Change the **Padding** to **5 px**.

11. Preview the topic.

Pets in the Office Policy¶

Pets... we love them. As a Super Simplistic Solutions employee, you are permitted to bring your pet to work every Friday, provided your pet is not on the banned list below and you follow a few, simple rules.¶

A Few Simple Rules¶

- Your pet bites, we bite you... and you pay the piper¶

- Your pet poops in the office, you clean it up immediately¶

- Just say NO to barking!!!!¶

- Your pet must be on a leash at all times when NOT in your office¶

- All pets, except Cats and Dogs, must always be in an approved cage or aquarium¶

Banned From the Office!¶

- All snakes¶

- Rodents¶

- Spiders¶

---

12. Close the preview.

13. Save and then close the project.

Notes

iCONLOGiC
"Skills and Drills" Learning

Module 6: Tags, Expressions, and Variables

In This Module You Will Learn About:

- Condition Tags, page 84
- Condition Expressions, page 89
- Dynamic Filters, page 93
- Variables, page 96
- Snippets, page 98

And You Will Learn To:

- Create a Condition Tag, page 84
- Apply a Condition Tag, page 86
- Create a Condition Expression, page 89
- Apply Topic-Level Tags, page 92
- Create Dynamic Content Filters, page 93
- Create a Variable, page 96
- Work With Snippets, page 98

Condition Tags

A project can easily contain thousands of topics. But what if you want to exclude specific topics from being generated? Using conditions, you can *tag* topics or selected topic content (such as words, phrases, images... even table rows). You can then create conditions that control which tagged content is generated. Using conditions, you can maintain one project but generate multiple outputs; each output can have unconditional content (content that was not tagged and potentially appears in every output) or unique content that was tagged and associated with a specific output.

Guided Activity 37: Create a Condition Tag

1. Open the **reuse_content** RoboHelp project file. (The project is located within the **RoboHelpProjects** folder.)

2. View the Condition Tag area.

   ☐ from the panel at the left, **Author** area, click **Condition Tags**

   In the Condition Tags area, notice there are already two build tags (Online and Print). These tags are default tags that appear in every new RoboHelp project. You can elect to use the existing tags, delete them, or ignore them. For this project, you'll be ignoring them and creating your own.

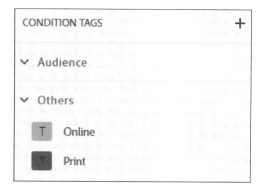

3. Create a Tag.

   ☐ at the top of the **Condition Tags** area, click the **New Tag** icon ⊞

   The Define Condition Tag dialog box opens.

   ☐ from the **Group** drop-down menu, choose **Audience**
   ☐ name the new tag **East Coast**

Group
Audience
Name
East_Coast

❏ choose any color you like as the **Background** and **Text**

Note: After you apply a tag to topic text and/or images (you'll do so very soon), you'll see the Background and Text colors. These colors allow you to quickly identify the tag that has been applied.

❏ click the **Done** button

The new Condition Tag is listed in the Condition Tags area within the Audience group.

> ∨ Audience
>
>   T   East_Coast

4. Create another Tag.

❏ at the top of the **Condition Tags** area, click the **New Tag** icon ⊞

The Define Condition Tag dialog box reopens.

❏ from the **Group** drop-down menu, choose **Audience**
❏ name the new tag **West Coast**

> **Define Condition Tag**
>
> Group
>
> Audience   ∨
>
> Name
>
> West_Coast

❏ choose any color you like as the **Background** and **Text**
❏ click the **Done** button

The Audience group in the Condition Tags area should look like this:

> ∨ Audience
>
>   T   East_Coast
>
>   T   West_Coast

5. Save the project.

Guided Activity 38: Apply a Condition Tag

1. Ensure that the **reuse_content** project is still open.

2. Apply a Condition Tag to text within a topic.

   ☐ open the **Our President** topic

The topic contains information about two presidents (AJ and Biff) so it's a bit hard to read.

Here's the scenario: Super Simplistic Solutions has gotten so big, the company has been split into two independent divisions: **East** and **West**. The two companies have different presidents (Biff in the East; AJ in the West) but share much of the same policies and procedures. Beyond personnel, the differences between the two companies are largely regional. For instance, the Eastern office isn't near the water; the Western office is located near a beach and employees routinely take their surfboards out during the lunch hour. Western management has recently installed surfboard racks. Information about the surfboard racks is relevant if you work in the West but not if you work in the East. You will use Condition Tags and Expressions to ensure that employees in the East see only information relevant to them; likewise for the employees in the West.

   ☐ in the **Our President** topic, highlight the phrase **Biff Bifferson**

   ☐ from the **Author** area at the left, select **Condition Tags**

   ☐ drag the **East_Coast** Condition Tag onto the selected text

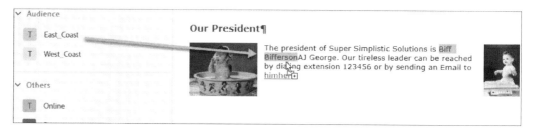

The Background and Text colors you selected when you created the condition appear on the selected text.

3. Apply a Condition Tag to more text within a topic.

   ❐ highlight the **Email** link for **him**

   ❐ from the **Condition Tags** area, drag the **East_Coast** Condition Tag onto the text

4. Save the project.

   Note: If you don't see the condition colors, choose **View > Show > Condition Tags** to make them appear.

Condition Tags Confidence Check

1. Select the picture at the right and apply the **East_Coast** Condition Tag to the picture.

2. Apply the **East_Coast** Condition Tag to the numbers **123**.

3. Apply the **West_Coast** Condition Tag to the following

   ❐ **AJ George**

   ❐ **456**

   ❐ the word **her** (the email link)

   ❐ the picture at the **left**.

   Note: You can remove a condition by right-clicking anything that has been tagged and choosing **Remove Condition Tag**.

4. Save the project.

5. Preview the topic.

6. From the **Filter** area at the right, select **East Coast**.

Information pertaining to AJ, who heads up the West Coast offices, disappears.

7. From the **Filter** area, deselect **East Coast**.

   Information pertaining to both presidents appears.

8. From the **Filter** area, select **West Coast**.

   Information pertaining to Biff, who heads up the East Coast offices, disappears.

Our President

 The president of Super Simplistic Solutions is AJ George. Our tirel leader can be reached by dialing extension 456 or by sending an Email to her.

9. Return to Author mode.

Condition Expressions

You have created two Condition Tags, applied them to topic text and images, and used the Preview feature to ensure the tags are displaying/hiding topic information correctly. To ensure you can create outputs that use the correct Condition Tags, you need to create condition expressions. An expression is a set of instructions that specify topics to include or exclude from an output. You can define a basic expression that excludes tags, or a complex expression with Boolean operators, such as AND, OR, and NOT.

Guided Activity 39: Create a Condition Expression

1. Ensure that the **reuse_content** project is still open.

2. Create a Condition Expression to be used for the West Coast output.

   ☐ from the panel at the left, select **Output**

   ☐ select **Condition Expressions**

   ☐ click the **New Condition Expression** icon ➕

   The **New Condition Expression** dialog box opens.

   ☐ name the expression **West Coast**

   ☐ click the **Done** button

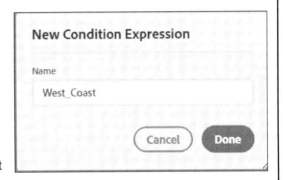

3. Add the West Coast tag to the expression.

   ☐ from the **A/B West Coast** area, drag the **West Coast** tag to the panel at the right

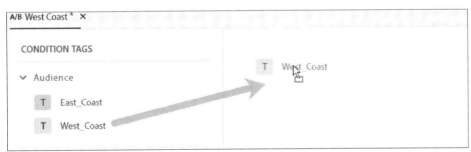

   ☐ from the drop-down menu, choose **Include**

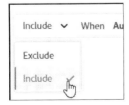

   Notice that the expression now reads "include when the audience is West Coast."

Expressions Confidence Check

1. Create a second Condition Expression named **East Coast** with content that will be **included** if the audience is made up of **East Coast** users.

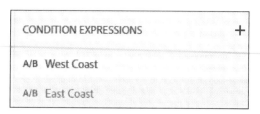

2. On the **Output** panel, select **Output Presets**.

3. Click the New Preset icon.

4. Choose **Frameless** from the **Type** drop-down menu, change the **Name** to **West Coast**, and then click the **Done** button.

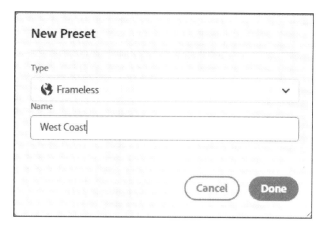

The new **West Coast** output opens for editing.

5. From the categories at the left, select **General**.

6. Change the Output path to **RoboHelp2019Data > output > Frameless**.

7. From the categories at the left, select **Content**.

8. From the **Condition Expression** drop-down menu, choose **West Coast**.

9. Save the project.

10. Generate the **West Coast** output and then view the output. (Prior to generating, ensure the Output Path is the **Frameless** folder within **RoboHelp2019Data > output** or you'll likely get an error.)

11. Open the **About This Guide** topic.

12. Click the **president** link.

Because you selected **West Coast** as the **Condition Expression**, Biff does not appear, and AJ is shown as the president.

13. Close the web browser and return to the RoboHelp project.

14. Duplicate the **West Coast** output and give the duplicate output the name **East Coast**.

15. Edit the **East Coast** output and, from the **Condition Expression** drop-down menu, choose **East Coast**.

16. Save the project.

17. Generate the **East Coast** output and then view the output. (Ensure the Output Path is the **Frameless** folder within **RoboHelp2109Data > output**)

18. Open the **About This Guide** topic.

19. Click the **president** link.

Because you selected **East Coast** as the **Condition Expression**, AJ does not appear, and Biff is the president.

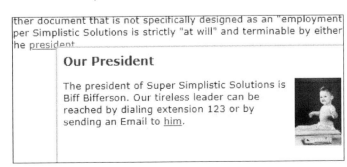

20. Close the web browser and return to the RoboHelp project.

Guided Activity 40: Apply Topic-Level Tags

1. Ensure that the **reuse_content** project is still open.

2. Apply a Condition Tag to a topic.

    ☐ at the left of the RoboHelp window, click **Author**

    ☐ from the **Contents** area, open the **General Office Information** folder

    ☐ right-click the **Surfboards** topic and choose **Properties**

    ☐ scroll down and expand **Condition Tags**

    ☐ from beneath **Topic Level**, click **Apply Tags**

    The Apply Condition Tags dialog box opens.

    ☐ from the Audience area, click **West Coast**

    The topic is added to the Audience list at the right.

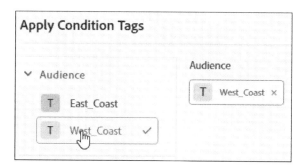

    ☐ click the **Apply** button

    By assigning the West Coast tag to the Surfboards topic, the topic appears *only* in the West Coast output. Because surfing is not a relevant topic for East Coasters, the topic does not need to appear in the East Coast output.

    ☐ click the **Apply** button again

    It's a subtle thing, but if you look at the Surfboards topic (in the General Office Information folder), an icon has been added to the topic indicating that a condition tag has been applied to the topic. (It's using the Background color you selected when you created the tag.)

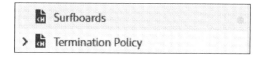

Dynamic Filters

You have learned how to create multiple Condition Tags and Condition Expressions and how to generate multiple outputs from one project (each containing potentially unique content). But what if you want to generate both outputs, combine them into one, and then let the users decide which output they want? During the activities that follow, you will create Dynamic Filters and then generate one output that contains information for both corporate locations. A user is then able to pick the appropriate content from a drop-down menu.

Guided Activity 41: Create Dynamic Content Filters

1. Ensure that the **reuse_content** project is still open.

2. Create a Dynamic Filter.

   ☐ from the **Output** area, select **Dynamic Content Filters**

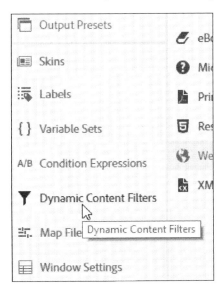

   ☐ click the **New Filter** icon ✛

   The New Filter dialog box opens.

   ☐ name the filter **Regions**

   ☐ click the **Done** button

3. Set Filter properties.

☐ in the **Title** area of the Regions filter, replace the placeholder text (Select the options) with **Choose Your Region**

☐ deselect **Allow multiple selection in groups**

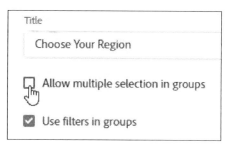

4. Add a Condition tag to the Filter.

☐ from the Condition Tags area, drag the **East_Coast** tag to where it says **Drag and drop tags here**.

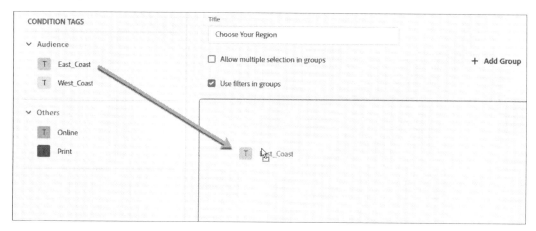

Dynamic Filters Confidence Check

1. Drag the **West_Coast** tag beneath the **East_Coast** tag.

2. Select the **East_Coast** tag and then click **Select by default**.

There are more employees working at the East Coast division than at the West Coast. By making the East_Coast filter the default, users will see the East Coast content by default but be able to switch to the West Coast content with a quick click.

3. From the **Output presets**, right-click **Responsive HTML5** and choose **Duplicate**.

4. Change the name of the new layout to **Dynamic** and then click the **Done** button.

5. Open the **Dynamic** output for editing and, on the **General** tab, ensure that the **Output path** is **RoboHelp2019Data/output/Responsive_HTML/** (browse to that folder now if necessary).

6. Select the **Content** tab.

7. From the **Condition Expression** drop-down menu, choose **<None>**.

8. From the **Dynamic Content Filter** drop-down menu, choose **Regions** (this is the Filter you created a moment ago)

9. Save the **Dynamic** output, **Generate**, and view the output.

10. On the TOC, open **General Office Information**.

    The East Coast content is the default. Because you added the **Surf Boards** topic to the West Coast filter, the Surf Boards topic is hidden from view because it is not relevant to East Coast employees.

11. On the TOC, select the **About This Guide** topic and then click the link for the **president**.

    Because this is the East Coast content and Biff is the president, Biff's information appears.

12. From the top of the Help System, click the **Filter** icon and then select **West Coast**.

    The change to the displayed content is as immediate as it is awesome. The TOC now includes the Surf Boards topic (in the General Office Information book.) In addition, the link to the Our President topic is now all about AJ, who is the President in the West Coast.

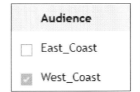

13. Close the browser window and return to the RoboHelp project.

Variables

Let's say you want to have your company name appear throughout a project. You could accomplish the task the old-fashioned way by typing the company name over and over again. Or you can create a Variable called CompanyName, whose definition is your actual company name. After creating the Variable, it's a simple matter of dragging the CompanyName Variable into any topic.

Now here's the cool part. Assume your company name appears throughout your project and you need to change it. Without the Variable, you would have to use the Find/Replace feature or manually find and edit every instance. Thanks to Variables, all you'll need to do is update the definition of the CompanyName Variable one time to change the displayed company name throughout the project.

Guided Activity 42: Create a Variable

1. Ensure that the **reuse_content** project is still open.

2. Create a Variable for the company name.

   ☐ from the **Author** area, click **Variables**

   ☐ click the **New Variable** icon ⊞

   The Define Variable dialog box opens.

   ☐ in the **Name** field, type **CompanyName**

   ☐ in the **Value** field, type **Sup. Simplistic Solutions**

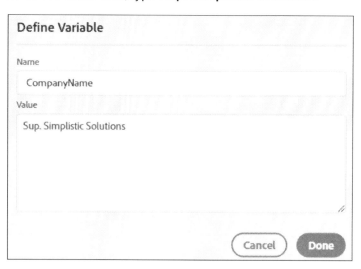

   ☐ click the **Done** button

   The new variable is listed in the Variables area.

3. Insert a Variable into a topic.

   ☐ from the **General Office Information** folder, open the **Nondiscrimination Policy** topic

   ☐ from the **Variables** area, drag the **CompanyName** variable into the topic (in front of the first word in the topic: **believes**)

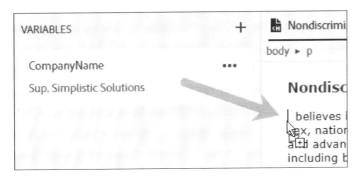

The Variable value appears in the topic. The color of the text is green, which is a visual indicator of a variable. Users will not see the text color.

4. Insert the Variable into another topic.

   ☐ open the **Absentee Policy** topic

   ☐ from the **Variables** area, drag the **CompanyName** variable into the topic (in the first sentence in front of the phrase **will permit**) and then press [**spacebar**]

5. Save the project.

6. Close all open topics.

7. Edit a Variable value.

   ☐ from the **Variables** area, double-click the **CompanyName** variable

   The Edit Variable dialog box opens.

   ☐ replace the word **Sup.** with **Super**

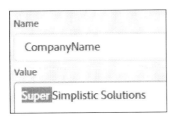

   ☐ click the **Done** button

8. Save the project.

9. Open either the **Nondiscrimination Policy** or **Absentee Policy** topic.

   The updated Variable content appears in both topics.

Snippets

Snippets are similar to variables but can contain multiple paragraphs (variable values can contain multiple lines, but not paragraphs), tables, and other higher-end HTML.

You can add Snippets to a project and later insert them into a desired topic. Like Variables, when you edit a Snippet shared by different topics, the changes to the Snippet are reflected in all the associated topics.

Guided Activity 43: Work With Snippets

1. Ensure that the **reuse_content** project is still open.

2. Create a Snippet.

   ☐ from the **Author** area at the left, click **Snippets**

   ☐ at the top right of the Snippets area, click the **New Snippet** icon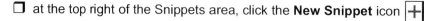

   The New Snippet dialog box opens.

   ☐ type **AbuseInfo** into the **Name** field

   ☐ in the **Description** field, type **Encourages employees to seek treatment.**

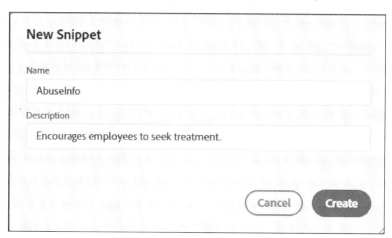

New Snippet

Name

AbuseInfo

Description

Encourages employees to seek treatment.

Cancel   Create

   ☐ click the **Create** button

   The Snippet opens in its own window, similar to creating a new topic.

   ☐ type the following into the Snippet window: **SSS recognizes that alcoholism and drug abuse are treatable illnesses, and encourages employees who may have alcohol or drug abuse problems to seek treatment for them. Any individual afflicted by alcoholism or drug dependency will have the same options as employees with other illnesses have to participate in prescribed treatment programs, including the use of paid leave and unpaid leave of absence.**

3. Save the project.

Snippets Confidence Check

1. Open the **Alcohol Policy** topic.

2. From the **Snippet** area, drag the **AbuseInfo** Snippet into the topic (just after the word beverages in the last paragraph.

   The text you typed into the Snippet appears within the topic.

Alcohol Policy

Super Simplistic Solutions does not permit or condone intoxication or drinking of alcoholic beverages on the premises of the company or at an employee's assigned place of duty on company time.

Such action will subject an employee to disciplinary action up to and including dismissal. It is Super Simplistic Solutions' policy to offer assistance to an employee whose work performance is adversely affected by repeated overindulgence in the use of alcoholic beverages.

See also: Drug Policy

SSS recognizes that alcoholism and drug abuse are treatable illnesses, and encourages employees who may have alcohol or drug abuse problems to seek treatment for them. Any individual afflicted by alcoholism or drug dependency will have the same options as employees with other illnesses have to participate in prescribed treatment programs, including the use of paid leave and unpaid leave of absence.

---

3. Add the **AbuseInfo** Snippet to the end of the **Drug Policy** topic.

4. Double-click the **AbuseInfo** Snippet in the Snippets area to open it for editing.

5. From near the end of the Snippet text, remove the following text: **to participate in prescribed treatment programs**.

6. From the beginning of the Snippet text, replace the letters **SSS** with the Variable **CompanyName**.

   > Super·Simplistic·Solutions·recogni
   > are·treatable·illnesses,·and·encou
   > alcohol·or·drug·abuse·problems·to
   > individual·afflicted·by·alcoholism·d

7. Save and close the Snippet.

8. Open both topics that are using the Snippet (Alcohol Policy and Drug Policy).

   Notice that the Snippet text has been updated in both topics (it now includes the CompanyName variable).

9. Save and then close the project.

Notes

iCONLOGiC

"Skills and Drills" Learning

Module 7: Tables, Indexes, Search, and Glossaries

In This Module You Will Learn About:

And You Will Learn To:

Tables

Tables, which are made up of cells (a rectangle that can contain data), columns (a vertical collection of cells) and rows (a horizontal collection of cells) allow you to organize data in an easy-to-read format. During the activities that follow, you will learn how to insert and edit tables—and how to work with Table Styles that make Table formatting a breeze.

Guided Activity 44: Insert a Table

1. Open the **tables_index** RoboHelp project file. (The project is located within the **RoboHelpProjects** folder.)

2. Insert a table into the Vacation Policy topic.

   ❏ open the **Vacation Policy** topic (the topic is located within the **Leave and Vacation** folder)

   ❏ click after the topic text **10,001 + 20 days** and press [**enter**] to create a new paragraph

   ❏ from the toolbar above the topic, click the **Insert Table** icon

   ❏ choose **4 rows** and **2 columns**

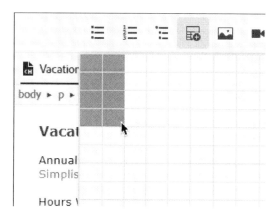

There is now an empty table just above the last paragraph in the topic.

3. Drag existing topic text into the table.

   ❏ from above the table, highlight the phrase **Hours Worked**

   ❏ drag the text into the **first** cell in the **first** row

Tables Confidence Check

1. Continue dragging topic content (the hours worked and the days allowed per year) into the table until your table looks like the picture below.

Vacation Policy¶

Annual vacation leave is based on the following schedule related to years of employment Simplistic Solutions.¶

Hours Worked	Days Allowed per Year
0 – 6000	10 days
6001 - 10,000	15 days
10,001 +	20 days

You are eligible to take vacation days earned after you have been paid for 1000 hours. Ea will be allowed to carry over into the next calendar year 120 hours of vacation. Any unus excess of 120 hours will be forfeited. Leave may be taken only after it is earned; no adva be approved. Use of vacation time is subject to management approval, and requests shou least 2 weeks in advance. Only persons who remain employed are eligible for vacation. U

2. Save the project.

Guided Activity 45: Work With Table Styles

1. Ensure that the **tables_index** project is still open.

2. Create a Table Style to use on all project tables.

   ❒ click within the table you created

   ❒ from above the topic, click the **table** tag to select the entire table

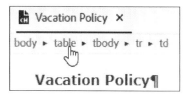

   ❒ from the **Properties** panel at the right, click the **Styles** tab

   ❒ from the drop-down menu choose **Table Styles**

   ❒ at the right of **Table Styles**, click the **Add Style** icon ⊞

   The Add Style dialog box opens.

   ❒ from the style list, scroll down and select **table**

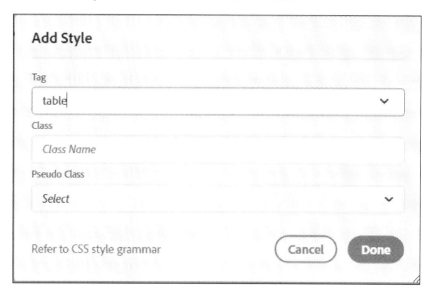

   ❒ click the **Done** button

   The policies style sheet you created during earlier lessons in this book opens. The **tables** style you added is listed in the Table Styles folder.

3. Change the font and font size used in the table.

   ❒ from the **Properties** panel, **Apply formatting to** drop-down menu, choose **Whole Table**

❒ from the **Font** drop-down menu, choose **Verdana**

❒ change the Font size to **10 pt**

4. **Close** and **save** the policies style sheet.

Your table, which is using the table style, has font and font size formatting that matches the rest of the topic content. During the Confidence Check that follows, you'll add space between the cell contents and space above and below the table.

Annual vacation leave is based on the following schedule related to years of employmen Simplistic Solutions.¶

Hours Worked	Days Allowed per Year
0 – 6000	10 days
6001 – 10,000	15 days
10,001 +	20 days

You are eligible to take vacation days earned after you have been paid for 1000 hours. I

Tables Confidence Check

1. Edit the **table** style.

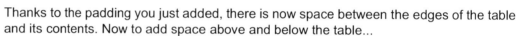

2. Change the **padding** for the Cells to **12 px**.

3. Save and close the style sheet.

   Thanks to the padding you just added, there is now space between the edges of the table and its contents. Now to add space above and below the table...

Hours Worked	Days Allowed per Year
0 – 6000	10 days
6001 - 10,000	15 days

4. Edit the **table** style again. This time, locate the Margin controls and add 20 px of space for the **top** and **bottom** margins.

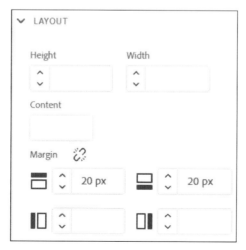

5. After saving the closing the style sheet, you should see ample white space both above and below the table.

Indexes

An index is a list of keywords that take users to project topics. Although often overlooked by novice Help authors, the index is the second most commonly used feature of a Help System (behind the Search feature).

Guided Activity 46: Add Index Keywords from Within a Topic

1. Ensure that the **tables_index** project is still open.

2. Add Index entries from within a topic.

   ☐ open the **About This Guide** topic (the topic is within the General Office Information folder)

   ☐ highlight the heading (About This Guide) and **copy** it to the clipboard

   ☐ from the **Properties** panel at the right, select the **Topic** tab

   ☐ expand the **Index** section

   ☐ click in the Index text field and **paste** the text you copied to the clipboard

   ☐ press [**enter**] to add the pasted text as an Index keyword

   ```
   ∨  INDEX

   ┌──────────────────────────────┐
   │ Index Keywords               │
   └──────────────────────────────┘
   ┌──────────────────────────┐
   │ About This Guide   ✕      │
   └──────────────────────────┘
   ```

   ☐ from within the topic, highlight the phrase **Super Simplistic Solutions** and **copy** it to the clipboard

   ☐ click in the Index text field and **paste** the text you copied to the clipboard

   ☐ press [**enter**] to add the pasted text as an Index keyword

3. Copy and paste the following keywords into the Index (or type the text manually).

   ☐ Policies and Procedures

   ☐ Employment Contract

   ☐ At Will

   Note: When you copy/paste the text as an Index Keyword, consider manually capitalizing the initial letters (which is typical of index entries).

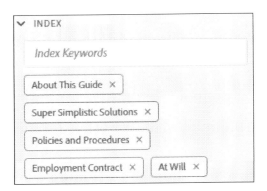

Guided Activity 47: Add Index Keywords on the Index Panel

1. Ensure that the **tables_index** project is still open.

2. Add an Index entry on the Index panel.

   ☐ from the panel at the left, **Author** area, click **Index**

   The keywords you added during the last activity appear in the Index.

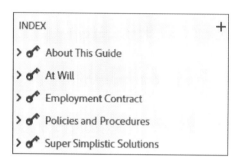

   ☐ from the top of the Index, click the **New Keyword** icon +

   ☐ type **Officers** and press [enter]

   The new Index keyword has been added but is not yet associated with any topics. Note there is no arrow to the right of the keyword. Arrows appear when a keyword is associated with one or more topics.

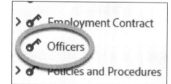

3. Associate topics with an Index keyword.

   ☐ right-click the **Officers** keyword and choose **Add Topic**

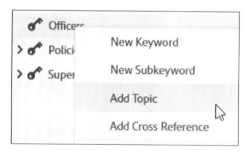

   The Add Topic dialog box opens.

   ☐ from the **Company Officers** folder, select **Human Resources**

   ☐ click the **Link** button

   The topic has been added beneath the Officers Index keyword.

Guided Activity 48: Edit Multiple Topic Properties

1. Ensure that the **tables_index** project is still open.

2. Use the Topic List pod to add multiple topics to an Index at one time.

   ❑ choose **View > Topic List**

   A list of all project topics appears.

   ❑ select **IS.htm**, **Our_President.htm**, and **webmaster.htm** (put checks in each topic box)

   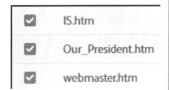

   ❑ right-click any of the selected topics and choose **Properties**

   The Multiple Topic Properties dialog box opens. Any change you make from here will affect all three selected topics.

   ❑ click in the **Index** text field and then select **Officers**

   Check your spelling carefully. Officers is an existing keyword. If you typed the keyword differently from the existing keyword, you'll end up with a new keyword.

   ❑ click the **Apply** button

3. Save the project.

4. Refresh the Topic List.

   ❑ from the top of the Topic List, click the **Refresh** icon

   In the **Index** column of the Topic List, notice that the word **yes** has been added (an indication that the three topics appear in the index at least one time).

5. On the Index itself, notice that the selected topics have been added to the Officers keyword and there's now an arrow (a chevron) to the left of the keyword.

   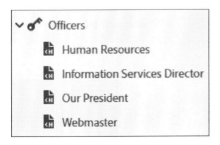

Index Confidence Check

1. Open the **Responsive HTML5** Output.

2. Change the **Title** to **Policies and Procedures**.

3. Change the Output path to **RoboHelp2019Data > output > Responsive_HTML**.

4. Generate the Responsive HTML5 Output.

5. Click the **Index** icon [A-Z] to see the Index you created.

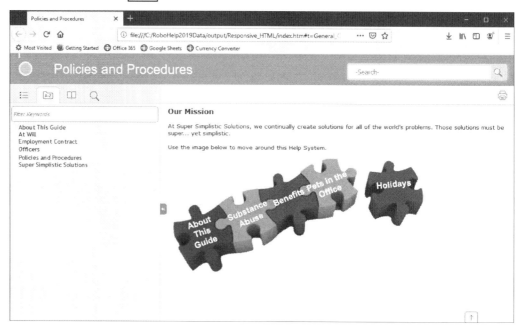

6. Close the browser and return to RoboHelp.

7. Go from topic to topic and add Index keywords as you see fit.

8. Use the **Topic List** to add Index keywords to multiple topics at the same time.

9. Generate Responsive HTML5 and observe your new Index entries in the output.

10. Close the browser and return to RoboHelp.

See Also Links

You have now learned about index entries and how to create them. Every index entry that you associate with a topic appears on the Index pane of the generated project. But there is a second type of keyword known as See Also. See Also keywords allow you to place related topics into one common group. See Also keywords do not appear on the Index when you generate the output. One popular way to get a See Also to appear is to use See Also Links.

In the next activity, you will create a See Also keyword and associate some topics with it. Then you will create a Link Control in a topic that tells the See Also links to appear in a topic.

Guided Activity 49: Create a See Also Keyword

1. Ensure that the **tables_index** project is still open.

2. Create a See Also keyword.

   ☐ from the panel at the left, **Author** area, click **See Also**

   ☐ from the top of the **See Also** panel, click the **New See Also Keyword** icon

   The **New See Also Keyword** dialog box opens.

   ☐ name the See Also Keyword **Managers**

   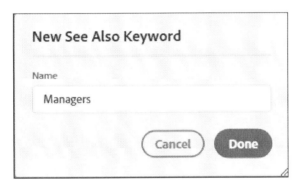

   ☐ click the **Done** button

3. Associate topics to a See Also Keyword.

   ☐ double-click the **Managers** See Also keyword you just added

   Two options appear beneath Manager: **Associated Topics** and **Used In Topics**.

   ☐ click the **Add Associated Topic** icon

   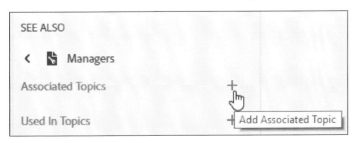

   The **Add Associated Topic** dialog box opens.

☐ from the **Company Officers** folder, select **Human Resources**

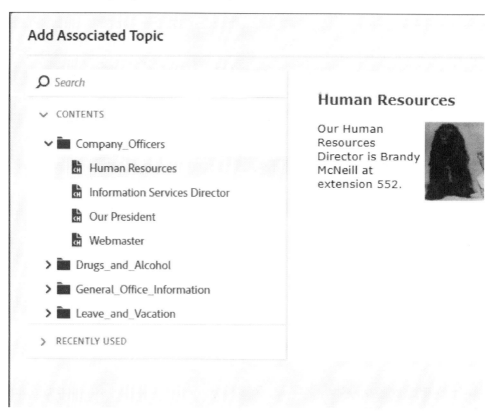

☐ click the **Link** button

The Human Resources topic appears in the Associated Topics area.

Index Confidence Check

1. Add the following three topics to the **Managers** See Also Keyword:

   ☐ Information Services Director

   ☐ Our President

   ☐ Webmaster

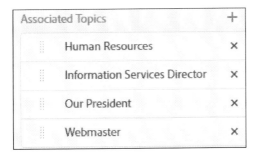

Associated Topics	+
⠿ Human Resources	✕
⠿ Information Services Director	✕
⠿ Our President	✕
⠿ Webmaster	✕

2. Add the four officers to the **Used In Topics** area.

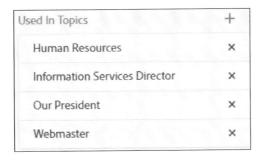

Used In Topics	+
Human Resources	✕
Information Services Director	✕
Our President	✕
Webmaster	✕

Now that you've created the See Also keyword (Managers), linked it to topics (the four officers), and then added it to four topics (also the officers), all that's left to do is add the See Also links within some of the topics. You'll then be able to test the links after generating Frameless.

Guided Activity 50: Insert a See Also Placeholder into a Topic

1. Ensure that the **tables_index** project is still open.

2. Open the **Our President** topic.

3. Insert a See Also Placeholder.

   ☐ click at the end of the text and press [**enter**] to create a new paragraph

   ☐ from the toolbar above the topic, click the **See Also Placeholder** icon

   The placeholder is added to the topic. Because you assigned the Managers See Also to this topic (and the other three managers), the placeholder loads the related topics when you generate output.

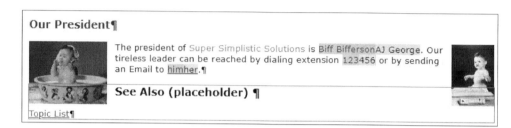

4. Open **Responsive HTML5** output.

5. On the **Content** tab, select **Regions** from the **Dynamic Content Filter** drop-down menu.

6. Save the project.

7. **Generate** and **View** the Output.

8. Click in the **Search** field, type **president** and press [**enter**].

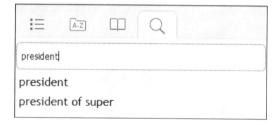

   The Help System is searched and topics containing the word "president" display in the results area (the results are ranked in order of relevance).

9. Click the first result (**Our President**) to open the Our President topic.

> Our President
>
> **president** of Super Simplistic Solutions is . Our tireless leader can be reached
>
> Company_Officers/Our_President.htm
>
> Information Services Director
>
> Human Resources Our **president** Webmaster
>
> Company_Officers/IS.htm

Thanks to the **Managers** See Also control, the topic contains links to the other managers. However, notice that the current topic, Our President, does not appear in the list of topics, even though Our President is one of the Associated Topics. Nice!

> **Our President**
>
> The president of Super Simplistic
> an Email to him.
>
> **See Also**
>
> Human Resources
> Information Services Director
> Webmaster

10. Select any of the topics in the list to open the topic (when you do, notice that the link to the topic you're in is automatically removed from the list of links).

11. Close the browser and return to the RoboHelp project.

Search

During the last activity, you used the Search feature to find a topic. You may have noticed that the Search results were ranked based on their relevance. If a word being searched appears in the title of a topic, its rank is higher than the word appearing in the body of a topic. In addition, a topic with the word appearing in a paragraph using a Heading 1 style ranks higher than the same word appearing in a paragraph using a Heading 2 style.

During the following activity, you will learn how to add search terms to a topic when those terms do not actually appear in the topic. Topics with custom search terms will appear higher in the search results than topics without these search terms set.

Guided Activity 51: Add Custom Search Terms

1. Ensure that the **tables_index** project is still open.

2. Open the **Human Resources** topic.

   There isn't much text in the topic, in fact, just 10 words (12 if you count the heading). Anyone searching for Brandy, McNeill, Human Resources, or Human would correctly find the topic. However, if someone searches for a word that is not physically in the topic, such as **conflict**, they won't find anything. Let's test that.

3. Generate Responsive HTML5 and View the output.

4. Use the Search field to search for **conflict**.

   No topics are found.

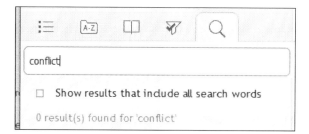

5. Close the web browser and return to the RoboHelp project.

6. Add a custom Search term to a topic's Properties.

   ☐ open the **Human Resources** topic

   ☐ from the **Properties** panel, click the **Topic** tab

   ☐ in the **Search** area, type **conflict** into the text field and then press [**enter**]

7. Save the project.

8. Generate **Responsive HTML5** and **View** the output.

9. Use Search to search for **conflict**.

    This time the Human Resources topic is found even though the word "conflict" is not actually within the topic.

    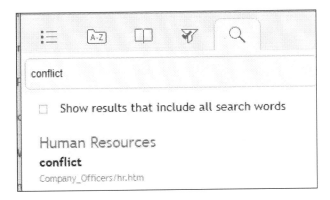

    Note: If you want to exclude a topic from appearing on the Search tab, you can go to the Search area for the topic's Properties and select **Exclude this topic from search**.

10. Close the browser and return to the RoboHelp project.

Guided Activity 52: Add a Search Synonym

1. Ensure that the **tables_index** project is still open.

2. Open the **Alcohol Policy** topic.

   This topic contains the word "Alcohol" in the heading. When searching for "alcohol" a user is sure to find this topic. However, one common misspelling of "alcohol" is "alchohol." If someone searches for "alchohol" they won't find topics. By adding a search synonym, you take misspelled search terms into account.

3. Create a search synonym.

   ☐ from the panel at the left, **Output** area, click **Synonyms**

   ☐ double-click **English (US)**

   ☐ in the **Word** column, type **alcohol**

   ☐ in the **Synonym** column, type **alchohol** and press **[enter]**

4. Save the project.

5. Generate **Responsive HTML5** and **View** the output.

6. Use the Search tab to search for **alchohol**.

   All topics with the text "alcohol" will be found even though the word **alchohol** was the Search term.

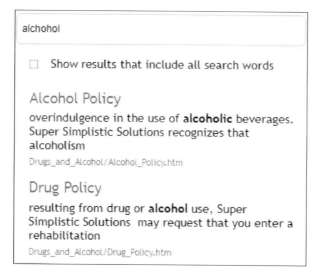

7. Close the browser, return to the RoboHelp project and close all open topics.

Glossaries

A glossary gives your users a list of words and their definitions related to content presented in your Help System. Most users rely heavily on both the Index and Search features. Because access to the Glossary is conveniently located next to both of those tools, it's a good bet that it gets plenty of use.

Guided Activity 53: Add Glossary Terms

1. Ensure that the **tables_index** project is still open.

2. View the Glossary.

   ☐ from the panel at the left, **Author** area, click **Glossary**

   ☐ double-click the existing Glossary (**policies**) to open it

   There are no glossary terms. You add glossary entries similarly to how you added index keywords earlier.

3. Add a New Term to a glossary.

   ☐ at the top of the policies Glossary, click the **New Term** icon ➕

   ☐ type **SSS** as the Term

   ☐ click in the **Definition** area and type **Super Simplistic Solutions**

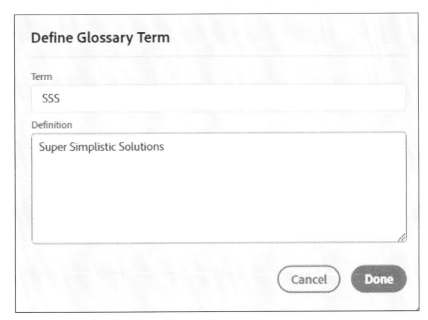

   ☐ click the **Done** button

4. Save the project.

Glossary Confidence Check

1. Add the following Glossary terms and definitions to the Glossary pod.

   EAP

   Employee Assistance Program

   ECT

   Earned Compensatory Time

2. Save the project.

3. Generate **Responsive HTML5** and **View** the output.

   Notice that there is now a **Glossary** tab.

4. Click the **Glossary** tab and spend a moment clicking on the Glossary Terms and reviewing the definitions that expand.

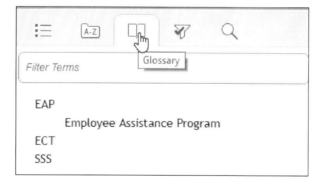

5. When finished, close the browser and return to the RoboHelp project.

6. Save and close the project.

iCONLOGiC
"Skills and Drills" Learning

Module 8: Skins and Master Pages

In This Module You Will Learn About:

And You Will Learn To:

Skins

As you've seen while creating content and generating outputs, there are quite a few layouts available on the Output panel from which to choose. Most of the Output Presets allow for a significant amount of customization. In fact, the icons, the colors, the fonts... just about everything about the appearance of an output is controlled by its Skin. Think of Skins as the clothing for your Help System.

Favicons and Default Topics

Favicons became popular several years ago. They are tiny images that appear to the left of a web address on browser tabs. In the images below, notice the IconLogic favicon to the left of the web address at iconlogic.com and the Amazon favicon for amazon.com.

The Default Topic is the topic that appears when users first access the Help System.

During the activities that follow, you'll create an output for Responsive HTML5 and edit the output by assigning both a favicon and default topic. Then you'll spend some time editing the Skin.

Guided Activity 54: Add a Favicon and Select a Default Topic

1. Using RoboHelp, open the **skins_masterpages.rhpj** RoboHelp project file.

2. Create an Output.

   ☐ on the **Output** panel, click **Output Presets**

   ☐ from **Output Presets**, click the **New Preset** icon ⊞

   The New Preset dialog box opens.

   ☐ from the **Type** drop-down menu, select **Responsive HTML5**

   ☐ name the preset **Policies Output**

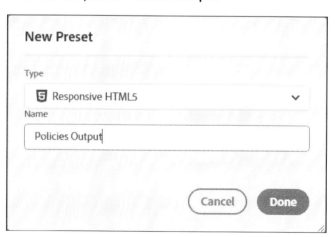

   ☐ click the **Done** button

   The new preset opens for editing.

---

3. Change the output Title and add a Favicon.

☐ with the **General** category selected, change the **Title** to **Policies & Procedures**

☐ in the **Favicon** area, click the **Select Favicon** icon 🔍

The **Select Favicon** dialog box opens.

☐ select **Local Files**

☐ click the **Browse** icon 🔍

☐ from **RoboHelp2019Data > images**, open **sss_favicon**

☐ click the **Select** button

```
Favicon
[icon]  C:/RoboHelp2019Data/RoboHelpProjects
```

4. Specify an Output location.

☐ from the **Output path** area, click the **Browse** icon 🔍

☐ from **RoboHelp2019Data > output**, open **Responsive_HTML** and then click the **Select Folder** button

```
Output Path
C:/RoboHelp2019Data/output/Responsive_HTML/            🔍
```

5. Specify a default topic.

☐ select the **Content** category

☐ from the **Default Topic** area, click the **Select Default Topic** icon 🔍

☐ from the **General Office Information** folder, select the **Mission Statement** topic

☐ click the **Select** button

6. Select a Dynamic Content Filter.

☐ from the **Dynamic Content Filter** drop-down menu, choose **Regions**

```
Dynamic Content Filter
Regions                                      ∨    ✏
```

Note: You learned about Dynamic Filters on page 93.

7. Select a Skin.

☐ select the **Layout** category

☐ from the **Skin** area, click the **Select from gallery** icon 🔍

The New Responsive HTML5 Skin dialog box opens. Skins are made up of the components that surround your Help System (the appearance of the TOC and Index icons for instance). The Skins have been designed to respond/reflow to the learner's display

↑NOTES↑

size and provide an optimum viewing experience. In the Preview area, you can see how content might look on a desktop, a mobile device, and a tablet.

❑ from the **Templates** list, **Charcoal_Grey**

❑ click the **Done** button

The Skin is added to the Output.

8. Save the project.

9. Generate and View the Policies Output. (Ensure the Output files go to the **Responsive_HTML5** output folder.)

10. Notice the Favicon image in the browser's page tab.

11. Resize the browser window smaller and smaller and notice how the navigation icons move and change as the window gets smaller. This is responsive design in action.

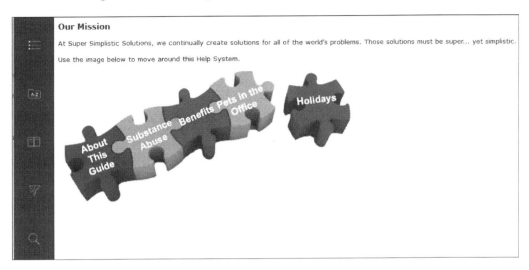

12. Close the browser and return to the RoboHelp project.

Guided Activity 55: Edit a Skin

1. Ensure that the **Skins and Master Slides** project is still open.

2. Open the **Policies Output** preset for editing.

3. Change the Home Icon used in the skin.

   ☐ select the **Layout** category

   ☐ from the **Skin** area, click the **Edit selected skin** icon

   The Skin Editor opens.

   ☐ from the list of **Skin Components**, select the **Header** category

   ☐ from the **Logo** area, click the **Browse** icon

   The **Insert Image** dialog box opens.

   ☐ click **Local Files**

   ☐ click the Browse button and, from **RoboHelp2019Data > images**, open **responsive_logo.gif**

   ☐ click the **Insert** button

   The image has been added to the Logo area and appears in the Header preview.

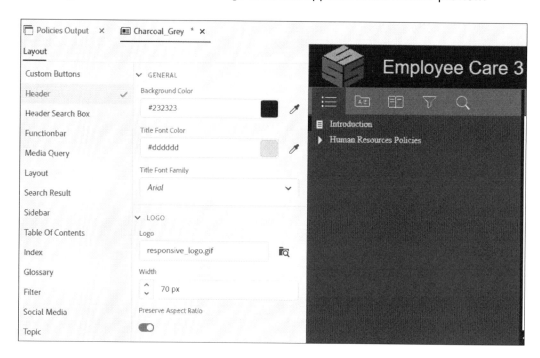

4. Close and Save the Charcoal_Grey Skin.

5. Generate and View the Policies output.

   The logo appears in the header and the header remains onscreen even if you make the browser window very small (to approximate what a phone user would see).

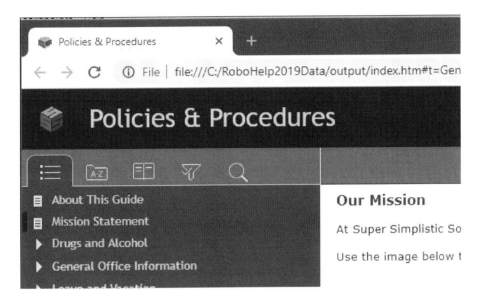

6. Close the browser and return to the RoboHelp project.

Skins Confidence Check

1. Edit the **Charcoal_Grey Skin** again, this time select the **Sidebar** option from the Layout list.

2. Change the **Background** color to any color you like.

3. At the top of the Skin, notice the icons for the different screen sizes (Desktop, Mobile, and Tablet).

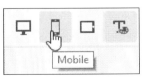

   Each of these icons has its own custom settings allowing you to provide a unique viewing experience for users on all kinds of screen sizes. If you'd like, make a few color changes/edits to the different screen sizes.

4. Close and save the Charcoal_Grey Skin.

5. Generate and View the **Policies** output to see your color changes.

6. Close the browser and return to the RoboHelp project.

Master Pages

A Master Page is a background that can be used on a topic. Master Pages can contain style sheets and page elements such as headers and footers.

Once created, a Master Page can quickly be attached to project topics. Should you make changes to the Master Page, any topics using the Master Page are updated. Using this concept, you can make a change on a Master Page and update thousands of topics in seconds.

Guided Activity 56: Create a Master Page

1. Ensure that the **skins_masterpages** project is still open.

2. Create a new Master Page

   ☐ from the panel at the left, **Author** area, click **Master Pages**

   ☐ from the top of the Master Pages panel, click the **New Master page** icon

   The New Master Page dialog box opens.

   ☐ **Name** the new Master Page **Copyright Notice in Footer**

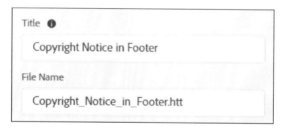

   ☐ click the **Create** button

   The new Master Page appears in the Master Pages area and automatically opens for editing. Notice that the Master Page contains an empty Header and Footer.

   MASTER PAGES

   📰 Copyright_Notice_in_Footer

¶

This is Body Placeholder text for your Master Page. Topics created using this Master Page will get this text by default. Replace text of this Body Placeholder with your default content for topics.¶

¶

Area outside this Body Placeholder represents the layout of the Master Page which will not be shown in the associated topics but will be present in the output. The Body Placeholder content will be replaced by actual topic content in the output.¶

¶

Use Master Page to define the layout of your topic in the output.¶

¶
----

3. Assign a style sheet to a Master Page.

☐ from the **Properties** panel at the right, select the **Topic** tab

☐ from the **Style Sheets** drop-down menu, choose **policies.css**

4. Insert a copyright symbol and some text into the Footer.

☐ in the topic, click within the **Footer**

☐ from the toolbar above the topic, click the **Insert Symbol** icon

☐ from the **Select Category** drop-down menu, choose **Special Characters**

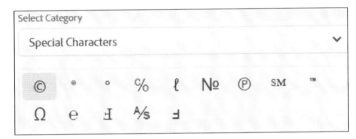

☐ click the **Copyright** symbol

☐ click the **Insert** button

☐ click the **Close** button

☐ press [**spacebar**] and type **Super Simplistic Solutions, All Rights Reserved**

5. Center the Footer text and add a line above the text.

☐ click to the left of the copyright symbol in the Footer

☐ on the **Properties** panel, select the **General** tab

☐ from the **Alignment** area, click the **Align Center** icon

☐ expand the **Border** area

☐ from the **Border Style** drop-down menu, choose **Solid**

☐ from the **Border** area, click the **Top Border** icon

The Footer should look like this:

Use Master Page to define the layout of your topic in the output.

© Super Simplistic Solutions, All Rights Reserved

6 Save the project.

7. Close the Master Page.

8. Apply a Master Page to a topic.

☐ open the **Special Benefits** topic

☐ from the **Properties** panel, select the **Topic** tab

☐ expand the **General** area

☐ from the **Master Page** drop-down menu, choose **Copyright Notice in Footer**

Master Page

Copyright_Notice_in_Footer ⌄

9. **Preview** the topic.

Notice that the footer you set up in the Master Page appears at the bottom of the topic.

Super Simplistic Solutions believes it is in the best interests of the employee, the employee's family, and the employer to provide an employee service that can provide help with complete confidentiality. Super Simplistic Solutions has contracted with the XYZ Employee Assistance Program of Uptown Hospital to provide this service. Their number is 703/555-1212. If you would like more information, please see the Human Resources Director.

© 2019-20 Super Simplistic Solutions

10. Return to **Author** mode.

11. Filter the Topic List.

☐ choose **View > Topic List**

☐ from the right of the Topic List, **Folder** drop-down menu, choose **Drugs and Alcohol**

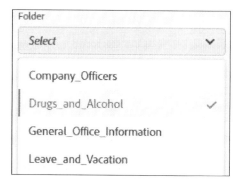

Folder

Select ⌄

Company_Officers

Drugs_and_Alcohol ✓

General_Office_Information

Leave_and_Vacation

Only the two topics in the Drugs and Alcohol folder are shown in the Topic List.

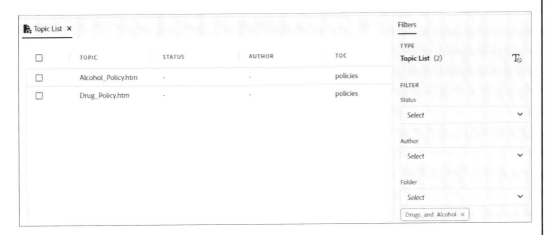

12. Apply the Master Page to more topics.

☐ in the **Topic List** window, select both the **Alcohol** and **Drug** Policy topics

☐ right-click the selected topics and choose **Properties**

The **Multiple Topics Properties** dialog box opens.

☐ from the **Master Page** drop-down menu, choose **Copyright Notice in Footer**

☐ click the **Apply** button

Both topics are now using the Copyright Notice in Footer Master Page.

13. Open the **Alcohol Policy** topic.

14. Preview the topic and confirm you can see the footer from containing the copyright notice.

15. Return to **Author** mode.

16. Save the project.

Guided Activity 57: Edit a Master Page

1. Ensure that the **skins_masterpages** project is still open.

2. Edit the footer on the Master Page.

   ☐ from the panel at the left, **Author** area, click **Master Pages**

   ☐ double-click the **Copyright Notice in Footer** Master Page (to open the Master Page for editing)

   ☐ click in the Footer

   ☐ click after the word **Solutions,** and type **Inc.**

   ☐ add a period after the phrase **All Rights Reserved**

   ---
   ur topic in the output.

   © Super Simplistic Solutions, Inc. All Rights Reserved.
   ---

3. Save and close the Master Page.

4. Open the **Alcohol Policy** topic.

5. Preview the topic.

   The topic displays the updated footer. In fact, any topics in your project using the Copyright Notice in Footer Master Page now have the updated footer.

6. Return to **Author** mode.

7. Save the project.

Master Page Confidence Check

1. Apply the **Copyright Notice in Footer** Master Page to the topics in the following two folders: **General Office Information** and **Leave and Vacation**.

2. Remove the Copyright Notice in Footer Master Page from the **Mission Statement** topic. (Show the topic's Properties and set the Master Page to **<None>**.)

3. Save the project.

4. Generate the Policies Output and then View the Output.

   All of the Help System topics, except Mission Statement, should now contain footers, and those footers should contain the corporate copyright notice.

5. Close the browser and return to the RoboHelp project.

6. Open the **Copyright Notice in Footer** Master Page for editing.

7. Click in the **Header**.

8. From the toolbar, click the **Insert Variables/Snippet/Fields** icon 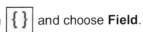 and choose **Field**.

9. From the **Field** list at the left, choose **Project Title**.

10. From the **Format** area, choose the first format (**Skins and Master Slides**) and then click the **Insert** button.

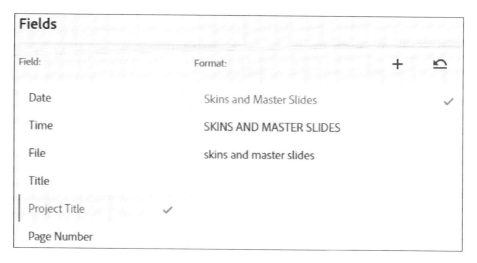

11. The current project's title is inserted into the Header.

12. Change the Paragraph alignment for the Header to **Right**.

13. Save and close the Master Page.

14. Open the **Alcohol Policy** topic.

15. Preview the topic to see the Project Title in the Header.

16. Return to Author mode.

17. Choose **File > Project Settings**.

18. Change the project's Title to **Policies and Procedures** and click the **Done** button.

    The updated Project Title field is updated on the **Copyright Notice in Footer** Master Page. All of the topics that are using the **Copyright Notice in Footer** Master Page instantly get the updated title.

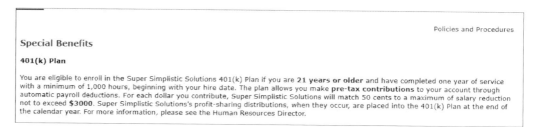

19. Save and close the project.

iCONLOGiC
"Skills and Drills" Learning

Module 9: Windows, Browsing, and CSH

In This Module You Will Learn About:

And You Will Learn To:

HTML Help Windows

Microsoft HTML Help isn't viewed via a web browser like Frameless our Responsive HTML5 outputs. HTML Help, using a program called the Help Viewer, opens in a specific location on the user's display and is set to a specific size and width. These weren't features you were asked to notice when you generated HTML Help earlier in this book, so it's likely you didn't. Nevertheless, you can control several HTML Help window features by creating a custom window and then attaching the window to the output prior to generating. In addition to controlling the placement and size of the window, you can add a search tab, browse sequence, and custom buttons to the Help window.

Guided Activity 58: Create a Custom Window

1. Open the **custom_app.rhpj** RoboHelp project file.

2. Create a new window.

   ☐ from the panel at the left, click **Output**

   ☐ click **Window Settings**

   ☐ from within the **Window Settings** area, click the **New Window Setting** icon ⊞

   The Window Setting dialog box opens.

   ☐ in the **Name** field, type **Super Simplistic Solutions Window**

   Window Setting

   Name

   Super Simplistic Solutions Window

   Cancel   Done

   ☐ click the **Done** button

   The new window's settings screen opens by default.

3. Set the Tri-pane Tabs and Windows options.

   ☐ expand the **Window Properties**

   ☐ from the **Tri-pane Tabs and Windows** area, ensure that **TOC & Index** is selected

   ☐ ensure that **Glossary** is selected

   You learned how to create a Glossary on page 119. The Glossary option ensures that the Glossary appears in the generated CHM file.

   ☐ ensure that **Search Tab** is selected

   ☐ ensure that **Browse Sequences** is selected

You will learn how to create a Browse Sequence soon. By selecting this option, the finished Browse Sequence appears in the Help window.

❑ ensure that the **Default Tab** is **Contents**

❑ ensure that the **Tab Position** is **Top**

Tri-Pane Tabs and Windows

☑ TOC & Index	☑ Search Tab	Default Tab: Contents ⌄
☐ Adv. Search	☐ Favorites	Tab Position: Top ⌄
☑ Glossary	☑ Browse Sequences	

4. Change the screen location and size of the new window.

❑ from the **Window Placement** area, change the **Top** to **25**

❑ change the **Left** to **25**

When you generate the Microsoft HTML Help output, the Help window appears 25 pixels from the top and left of the users' display.

❑ change the **Height** to **580**

❑ change the **Width** to **970**

Window Placement

25 px

25 px

Window Placement

⬛ 25 px	↕ 580 px	
▯ 25 px	↔ 970 px	

5. Set the Tri-pane options.

❑ from the **Tri-pane Options** area at the bottom left of the window, ensure **Auto-synchronize TOC** is selected

The Auto-synchronize TOC option synchronizes the left and right panes of your generated Help System so that selected books or pages on the TOC and topics match as the Help System is used.

❑ select **Remember Window Size and Position**

Tri-Pane Options

☐ Hide Nav Pane on Startup	Nav Panel Width 0
☑ Auto-synchronize TOC	
☑ Remember window size and position	
☐ Auto-show/hide Nav Pane	

NOTES

You are controlling the exact size and display position of the Help window. If users move or resize the window after it opens on their display, **Remember Window Size and Position** ensures that the Help window remembers the users' settings and puts the window in the same place the next time they open the Help System.

6. Add a Stop button.

    ❏ from the **Buttons** area, select **Stop** (turn the option on)

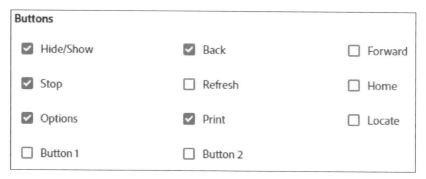

This option adds a Stop button to the Help window that instantly stops a page from loading into the Help System,.

7. Add a custom button, set a target URL for a button, and set it to take users to the Super Simplistic Solutions website.

    ❏ from the **Buttons** area, select **Button 1**

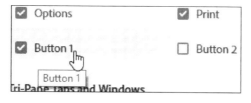

    ❏ expand the **Destinations** area

    ❏ in **Button 1 Label** field, type **Website**

    ❏ in the **Custom Button 1 URL** field, type **http://www.supersimplisticsolutions.com**

8. Save and close the Super Simplistic Solutions Window settings.

    Next you will tell RoboHelp to use the Super Simplistic Solutions window when you next generate Microsoft HTML Help.

9. Edit the Microsoft HTML Help preset's Title, Output location, and CHM file name.

☐ from the panel at the left, **Output** area, click **Output Presets**

☐ double-click **Microsoft HTML Help** to open its properties

☐ click the **General** category

☐ in the **Title** area, change the Title to **Policies and Procedures**

☐ in the **Output Path** area, browse to and select **RoboHelp2019Data > outputs > HTML_Help**

☐ change the name of the CHM File to **policies.chm**

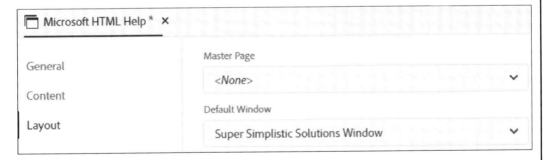

10. Edit the preset so that it uses the Super Simplistic Solutions Window.

☐ select the **Layout** category

☐ from the Default Window drop-down menu, choose **Super Simplistic Solutions Window**

11. Save and close the Output Preset.

Help Window Confidence Check

1. Generate Microsoft HTML Help and View the Output.

   Notice the position and size of the Help window.

2. Close the Help window and return to RoboHelp

3. Edit the **Super Simplistic Solutions** Window Placement Properties.

   ☐ Change the **Top** and **Left** Placement to **36**.

   ☐ Change the Window **Height** to **600**.

   ☐ Change the Window **Width** to **900**.

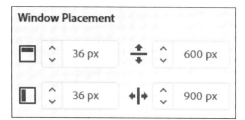

4. Deselect **Remember Window Size and Position**.

5. Save and close the Window Properties dialog box.

6. Generate Microsoft HTML Help again and View the Output.

   The resulting Help window should be smaller than before.

   Note: If you hadn't deselected **Remember Window Size and Position**, the size of your Help window would not have changed because you already viewed the window at the larger size.

7. Close the Help window and return to the RoboHelp project.

Browse Sequences

You can create a browse sequence for Responsive HTML5, HTML Help and Frameless. A browse sequence gives your users the freedom to move forward and backward through your topics in an order you create. The browse order can be based on anything you think might improve the usability of your project.

In this lesson, you will learn how to use the Browse Sequence Editor to create a browse sequence. Keep in mind that only topics and bookmarks included in your project can be used and although you will be creating only one browse sequence in this activity, you can have multiple browse sequences.

Guided Activity 59: Create a Browse Sequence

1. Ensure that the **Windows, Browsing, and CSH** project is still open.

2. Create a Browse Sequence.

   ❑ from the panel at the left, **Author** area, click **Browse Sequences**

   ❑ click the **New Browse Sequence** icon ⊞

   The New Browse Sequence dialog box opens.

   ❑ name the Browse Sequence **Managers**

   ❑ click the **Done** button

   The topic area opens.

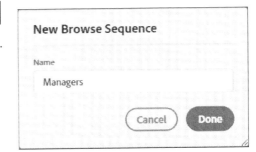

3. Add a topic to the browse sequence.

   ❑ from the **Contents** area, open the **Company Officers** folder

   ❑ drag the **Our President** into the Browse Sequence area

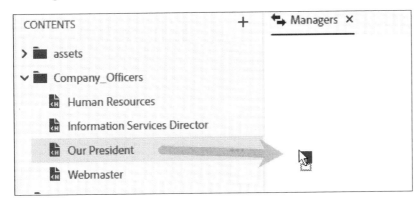

Browse Sequence Confidence Check

1. Add the remaining officers to the **Managers** browse sequence.

   As you add topics, keep the following in mind: (1) If you want to change the order of the browse sequence, use the Move icons to move the topics up or down; (2) if you want to remove a topic from the sequence, right-click and choose Delete.

2. Save and close the Browse Sequence.

3. From the panel at the left, **Output** area, edit the **Policies** Output Preset.

4. On the **General** tab, Ensure the Output is going to **RoboHelp2019Data > output > Responsive_HTML**.

5. From the **Content** category, select **Managers** from the **Browse Sequence** drop-down menu.

6. Save and close the preset.

7. Generate **Policies** and View the Output.

8. Use the **Search** feature to find and open the **Our President** topic.

9. Use the **Next** icons to move through the Browse Sequence.

10. Close the browser and return to the RoboHelp project.

Application Help

Up until now, your generated outputs have been Standalone Help Systems, meaning that anyone can double-click the generated CHM file (if you generated HTML Help) or the Start Page (if you generated Frameless or Responsive HTML5), and the Help System opens on his or her computer.

Application Help means that your generated output is intended to work from within a program. There isn't much you have to do to go from Standalone Help to Application Help, except hand the generated output to your application developer. From there, the application developer programs the application to open your generated and published Help System when the user clicks a Help link or icon.

To demonstrate Application Help, a web application is included within the **webapp** folder called **SimpleWebApplication**. The web application is looking for the Policies and Procedures Help System that you created during the previous modules in this book. When one application attempts to communicate with another, the interaction is called an API call (API meaning Application Programming Interface).

> **Note:** When testing help locally, use Google Chrome or Mozilla Firefox. Microsoft Edge and Internet Explorer do not work well. After you have uploaded the Help System to a web server, any browser can be used.

Guided Activity 60: Test an API Call for Help

1. Minimize RoboHelp.

2. Review the folder containing the published Help System files.

   ☐ using Windows Explorer, open the **RoboHelp2019Data** folder

   ☐ open the **webapp** folder

   There's not much within the webapp folder. There are a few folders and a web page (named SimpleWebApplication.htm) that I created using basic HTML tags. The web page is communicating with the other assets within the webapp folder. The most important folder, from your perspective, is the **helpsystem** folder.

   > helpsystem
   > images
   > policies.css
   > RoboHelp_CSH.js
   > SimpleWebApplication.htm

3. Open a web application and test the link to the Help System.

   ☐ double-click **SimpleWebApplication.htm** to open the application in your default web browser

   I added a link on the web page that is looking for a Help System similar to the one you've been building throughout this book. Because the generated output files have not been **published** into the **helpsystem** folder, the link to the Help System on the web page fails when clicked. You'll see that problem next when you attempt to get help from within the web application.

4. Attempt to get help from within the web application.

☐ in the **second paragraph**, click the link (the word **here**)

> If you click here, you will start the Help sy
> window than to the **target=_blank** tag.

The Help System does not open because you haven't yet published the RoboHelp output into the **helpsystem** folder.

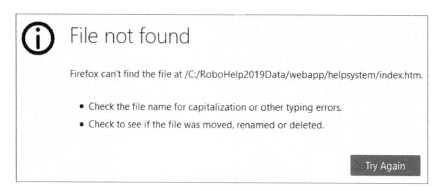

ⓘ File not found

Firefox can't find the file at /C:/RoboHelp2019Data/webapp/helpsystem/index.htm.

• Check the file name for capitalization or other typing errors.
• Check to see if the file was moved, renamed or deleted.

Try Again

☐ close the **File not found** window/tab and return to the **SimpleWebApplication** page

5. View an application's source code.

☐ using your mouse, point to (but don't click) the **link** in the **second paragraph** (the word **here**)

In the status bar at the bottom of the browser window, the HTML tag that links the web application to the Help System appears.

> file:///C:/RoboHelp2019Data/webapp/helpsystem/index.htm

You do not have to be an HTML expert to get a feel for the code. The link is looking within the webapp **helpsystem** folder for a specific file named **index.htm**. (Index.htm is the Start Page for the entire Help System, not a topic that you created. The Start Page is automatically created each time you generate the Frameless output.)

Once the Help System has been published to the **helpsystem** folder (you will learn how to publish during the next activity), the **index.htm** file exists and the Help System opens when the word **here** is clicked.

6. Close or minimize the browser window.

7. Open the **helpsystem** folder.

Because you have not yet published, the helpsystem folder is empty, which explains the reason the API call from the web page for the index.htm file failed. During the next activity, you will publish the project to the **helpsystem** folder and retest the API call.

8. Return to RoboHelp.

Publishing

You've generated your Help System multiple times during the activities in this book. When you generate an output, the generated files go into an output folder on your computer. To make the generated files available to your users, you need to copy the files to a shared location (typically a corporate web server or Intranet). Assuming users know the URL of the Help System's Start Page (the Start page is typically named index.htm and is created every time you generate), your job is done.

The most efficient way to get your generated content to a shared location is by **Publishing**. When your output files are published, RoboHelp copies the output files to the server for you. The first time you publish the project could take some time. However, after you edit the project, Generate, and then Publish, only the edited content (and required support files) is republished making the Publish process far faster than copying and pasting generated output to a shared location.

Guided Activity 61: Publish an Output

1. Ensure that the **Windows, Browsing, and CSH** project is still open.

2. Create a Publish Profile.

   ❐ from among the **Output Presets**, double-click the **Policies Output** Preset to open it for editing

   ❐ from the **General** category, ensure the **Output Path** is **RoboHelp2019Data > output > Responsive_HTML** (if not, change the path now)

   Output Path

   C:/RoboHelp2019Data/output/Responsive_HTML/

   ❐ select the **Publish** category

   ❐ click the **Publish Profiles** icon ⚙

   The Publish Profiles dialog box opens.

   ❐ click the **Create a new Profile** icon ➕

   You can choose from among the following Server Types: FTP, SFTP, File System, SharePoint Online, and RoboHelp Server. **FTP:** File Transfer Protocol uses a TCP/IP network that allows a user to *quickly* transfer large files from one computer to another over the Internet. **SFTP:** This is a secure version of FTP. **File System:** This is a great option if you want to publish your files to a network drive. **SharePoint Online**: A cloud-based service that helps organizations share and collaborate with colleagues and customers. **RoboHelp Server:** If you have Adobe RoboHelp Server (sold separately from RoboHelp) it extends the capabilities of RoboHelp. For instance, you can merge multiple projects into a unified information system.

   ❐ from the **Server Type** drop-down menu, choose **File System**

   Server Type

   File System

☐ in the **Name** area, type **Publish to WebApp**

Name

Publish to WebApp

☐ from the **Destination Path** area, click the **Change** icon

The **Select a Folder** dialog box opens.

☐ navigate to **RoboHelp2019Data > webapp > helpsystem**

Destination Path

C:/RoboHelp2019Data/webapp/helpsystem/

Notice that the target for the Published output is different from the Output Path for generated content. When you Generate output, all of the necessary Help System files are created within a folder on your computer. However, your users do not have access to the content unless you copy that content to a shared server. When you Publish, the generated content is copied to that shared location (typically a web server).

☐ click the **Save** button

Your new "server" now appears in the list of Servers.

	PROFILENAME	ADDRESS	UPLOAD LOCATION
☐	Publish to WebApp	-	C:/RoboHelp2019Data/webapp/helpsystem/

Publish Options

☐ select **Publish to WebApp**

☑	SERVERNAME
☑	Publish to WebApp

3. Save the preset.

4. Generate and then Publish the output files.

☐ generate the **Policies Output**

The output is created in the output folder as always.

☐ right-click the **Policies Output** preset and choose **Publish**

The output files are published (copied) to the **helpsystem** folder on your hard drive.

Publishing Confidence Check

1. Minimize RoboHelp, navigate to the **RoboHelp2019Data** folder, and open the **webapp** folder.

2. Open the **helpsystem** folder to see the published output files.

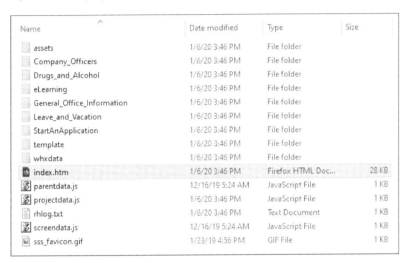

Name	Date modified	Type	Size
assets	1/6/20 3:46 PM	File folder	
Company_Officers	1/6/20 3:46 PM	File folder	
Drugs_and_Alcohol	1/6/20 3:46 PM	File folder	
eLearning	1/6/20 3:46 PM	File folder	
General_Office_Information	1/6/20 3:46 PM	File folder	
Leave_and_Vacation	1/6/20 3:46 PM	File folder	
StartAnApplication	1/6/20 3:46 PM	File folder	
template	1/6/20 3:46 PM	File folder	
whxdata	1/6/20 3:46 PM	File folder	
index.htm	1/6/20 3:46 PM	Firefox HTML Doc...	28 KB
parentdata.js	12/16/19 5:24 AM	JavaScript File	1 KB
projectdata.js	1/6/20 3:46 PM	JavaScript File	1 KB
rhlog.txt	1/6/20 3:46 PM	Text Document	1 KB
screendata.js	12/16/19 5:24 AM	JavaScript File	1 KB
sss_favicon.gif	1/23/19 4:56 PM	GIF File	1 KB

3. Go back to the **webapp** folder and reopen **SimpleWebApplication** in your web browser.

4. Click the link to the word "here."

This time the Help System that you just published to the "server" opens. Congratulations! You are now a published Help author!

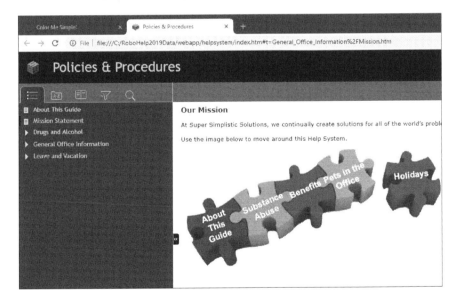

Note: If the published Help System did not open when you clicked the word "here," the issue is likely your web browser (some browsers act cranky when you test items such as links locally). If you have an alternative web browser installed on your computer, open **SimpleWebApplication** there and retest the link. As mentioned earlier, Mozilla Firefox works best when testing Help Systems locally; Internet Explorer historically causes the most trouble.

5. Close the Help System tab (or window). Keep **SimpleWebApplication.htm** open.

Context Sensitive Help

Context Sensitive Help (CSH) allows users to get help about specific areas of a program. Users can quickly get help without having to use the Help System's TOC, Index, or Search.

Here is how context sensitive help works: To make a topic context sensitive, the topic needs a unique topic ID and a map number. This information is stored in a **map file**. The application's programmer can (and most probably will) create the map file (also known as an **H** or **HH** file). Although just about any word processor can be used to create the map file, many programmers still use NotePad.

Here's an example of a map file entry: **#define ID_AboutSSS 5001**. The text **ID_AboutSSS** is the topic ID; **5001** is the map number.

After the programmer is finished with the map file, import the map file into your project. Then match the topics in your project with the IDs from the map file. After that, Generate the project and Publish.

In the next few activities, you will review the areas of the Simple Web Application that are meant to be context sensitive, create a map file in RoboHelp, and assign map numbers to a few topics.

Guided Activity 62: Review CSH Source Code

1. Attempt to get Context Sensitive Help.

   ☐ still working within the **SimpleWebApplication.htm** web application, click the link **Open just the Leave Policy** topic

   The way the developer designed **SimpleWebApplication**, the link you just clicked is supposed to start the Help System and then open just the **Leave Policy** topic in its own window. Instead, the entire Help System is started, and the Welcome topic opens. If you were the user looking for information on the Leave Policy, you would now have to manually search for the content.

2. Close the Help window but leave SimpleWebApplication.htm open.

3. Try to get additional Context Sensitive Help.

   ☐ click the link **Open just the Payroll Policy topic**

   The Help System starts again, but the Payroll Policy topic does not appear.

4. Close the Help window (or tab) but leave the SimpleWebApplication.htm page open in your browser so you can review some HTML code in the next step.

5. View the source code.

   ☐ point to (but don't click) the **Open just the Leave Policy topic** link

   HTML code displays in the browser's status bar (in most browsers, the status bar is located at the bottom of the browser window).

   Open just the **Leave Policy** topic

   Open just the **Payroll Policy** topic

   javascript:RH_ShowResponsiveHelpWithMapNo('helpsystem/index.htm', '', 45)

In the HTML code, the text "javascript" causes the JavaScript file named RH_ShowHelp to activate. The next bit of text ('helpsystem/index.htm) is what tells the Help System to open.

```
javascript:RH_ShowResponsiveHelpWithMapNo('helpsystem/index.htm', '', 45)
```

Finally, the last bit of text (, **45**) is what tells the Help System to display the topic with map ID number **45**. Soon you will assign Map ID **45** to the **Leave Policy** topic.

6. View another source code.

    ☐ using your browser, point to (but don't click) the **Open just the Payroll Policy topic** link

```
javascript:RH_ShowResponsiveHelpWithMapNo('helpsystem/index.htm', '', 46)
```

The end of the text (, **46**) is what tells the Help System to display the topic with map ID number **46**. Soon you will assign Map ID **46** to the **Payroll Policy** topic.

7. Leave SimpleWebApplication.htm open and return to the RoboHelp project.

Guided Activity 63: Create a Map File and Assign Map IDs

1. Ensure that the **Windows, Browsing, and CSH** project is still open.

2. Create a Map file.

   ☐ from the panel at the left, **Output** area, click **Map Files**

   ☐ click the **New Map File** icon ⊞ and choose **New Map File**

   The **New Map File** dialog box opens.

   ☐ type **CSHMap**

   ☐ click the **Done** button

   The new map file has been created within the Map Files area.

3. Assign a default Map ID to a topic.

   ☐ from the **CSHMap** area, open the **Leave and Vacation** folder

   ☐ drag the **Leave Policy** topic into the Drag and Drop area

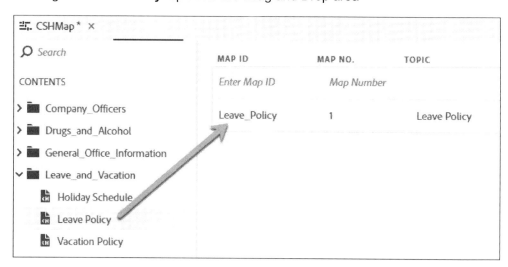

The **Leave Policy** topic is automatically assigned Map Number **1**. You need to change the number to **45** so it matches the reference in the web application's source code.

4. Edit a Map Number.

   ☐ in the **Map ID** area, double-click the existing Map Number (the number **1**) and change it to **45**

Maps Confidence Check

1. Add the **Payroll Policy** topic to the Map file.

2. Change the Map Number for the Payroll Policy to **46**.

Leave_Policy	45
Payroll_Policy	46

3. Save the project.

   Note: You've been prompted to save your work several times throughout this book. Reminding you to save isn't me encouraging good saving habits (and helping you prevent lost work... not that there's anything wrong with that). Instead, if you don't save the project assets frequently, changes to such things as Map Numbers don't always appear in other areas within RoboHelp.

4. Open the **Policies Output** Preset for editing.

5. Select the **Content** category, **Map Files** drop-down menu, choose **CSHMap**. (This is the map file you just created. If you had not saved the project as instructed above, the Map File would not be listed in the Map Files drop-down menu.)

Map Files

Select

CSHMap ×

6. Save the changes to the Preset.

7. **Generate** the output and **Publish Policies Output** Preset.

8. Return to the **SimpleWebApplication.htm** window.

9. Reload/Refresh the SimpleWebApplication web page.

10. Test the links to the **Leave** and **Payroll Policy** topics.

    Clicking either link should result in the topic appearing in the Help System.

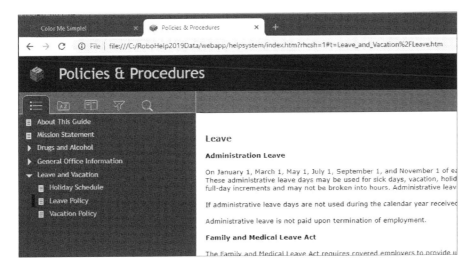

11. When finished, close the browser, return to RoboHelp, and close the project.

Notes

Index

NOTES

Made in the USA
Columbia, SC
03 February 2021